HAUNTED
CHELMSFORD

HAUNTED CHELMSFORD

Jason Day

The
History
Press

For my girls, Kelly and Abigail Day. You are my world.

Also for Mr and Mrs Day (Simon and Alison). Congratulations, 7 July 2012.

First published 2012

The History Press
The Mill, Brimscombe Port
Stroud, Gloucestershire, GL5 2QG
www.thehistorypress.co.uk

© Jason Day 2012

The right of Jason Day to be identified as the Author
of this work has been asserted in accordance with the
Copyrights, Designs and Patents Act 1988.

British Library Cataloguing in Publication Data.
A catalogue record for this book is available from the British Library.

ISBN 978 0 7524 6221 9

Typesetting and origination by The History Press
Printed in Great Britain

Contents

Acknowledgements

I would like to thank the following people for their help, support, patience and hard work in writing this book. Thank you to Cate Ludlow and The History Press; without whom the book would not have been possible. Also, thank you to my family for their love and tireless support of my work. Further thanks go to my wife Kelly Day (photos) and Tracie Wayling (illustrations), without your brilliant contributions the book would not have been possible either. I would also like to thank Alison White, Mick Cash, Pat Balcombe, Colin Brown, Derek Kelly, Gary Day, the Essex Ghost Hunting Team and the staff of Chelmsford Prison, both past and present.

Big thanks also to the staff of Broomfield Hospital, Maternity and Labour ward, Chelmsford; and the staff of the Royal London Hospital, Constance Green ward. Thanks also go out to Joan at the Sick Children's Trust, Stevenson House, for all her support over the last year. I should also like to thank those who have been brave enough to come forward with stories of their paranormal encounters in and around the Chelmsford area and have allowed me to share them with you. Special thanks also go to the spirits that have managed to manifest themselves one way or another; this book will let even more people know you are out there. Finally a big thank you to you the reader, I hope you enjoy the book.

About the Author

Writer and broadcaster Jason Day was born and raised in Scunthorpe, where he lived for nearly thirty years until moving to Essex. Jason was the longest serving feature writer for *Paranormal* magazine (March 2006-January 2008), the largest monthly paranormal publication of its kind in the UK at the time, writing over twenty articles during that period. He has also been a regular contributor to paranormal publications such as *FATE* magazine in the USA (the longest running paranormal magazine in the world) and *Ghost Voices* magazine in the UK. Jason also works with others in the written media, including some very prominent names in the paranormal community. His first book, *It's Only A Movie. Isn't It?* was released on 1 May 2010. Jason has since gone on to write *Haunted Scunthorpe* (October 2010, The History Press), *Paranormal Essex* (March 2011, The History Press) and *Haunted Grimsby* (November 2011, The History Press).

His interest in the paranormal was sparked by his love of film and passion for reading. Jason grew up on a staple diet of 'Hammer Horror' movies and the written works of Peter Underwood, Dr Hans Holzer and Harry Price. With the advent of television shows such as *Arthur C. Clarke's Mysterious World* and *Strange But True*, Jason was hooked. He decided to begin researching and investigating cases of the paranormal for himself and the fuse was lit.

Jason's experience working in the paranormal field has been varied, ranging from being a regular co-host on the *Friday Night Paranormal Show* on Pulse Talk Radio, to being the featured article writer for the paranormal reference website www.ghostdatabase.co.uk. Jason is also the chief consultant for the Famously Haunted Awards organisation on MySpace. He has been a guest on several radio shows, appeared at various paranormal events and given lectures about his work within the paranormal field and the subject of the paranormal in general.

Jason also hosted *The White Noise Paranormal Radio Show* online and has interviewed such figures in the paranormal community as James Randi, Dr Ciaran O'Keeffe, Derek Acorah, Lorraine Warren, Nick Pope, Stanton Friedman, Richard Wiseman, Ian Lawman, Jason Karl and Richard Felix. Running for Chelmsford is located in the county of Essex, within

Below: *The infamous witch's stone in Great Leighs. (Photograph by Kelly Day)*

Above: *Jason Day at St Anne's Castle Inn, the location of one of Chelmsford's most famous hauntings. (Photograph by Kelly Day)*

Official White Noise Radio Show Website (www.whitenoiseparanormalradio.co.uk). Jason and the show won two awards at the International Paranormal Acknowledgment Awards 2009. Jason was named Best International Paranormal Radio Show Host and The White Noise Paranormal Radio Show was voted Best International Paranormal Radio Program.

In early 2010, Jason began working with Phantom Encounters Limited, an events company offering a variety of paranormal experiences to the public, ranging from ghost hunts to UFO sky watches and monster hunts. Phantom Encounters also host Paranormal Lecture Series and Corporate Events. You can find out more about Phantom Encounters events at www.phantomencounters.co.uk.

One of three founding members of a small not for profit paranormal investigation team, based in Essex, by the name of SPIRIT (Society for Paranormal Investigation, Research, Information & Truth – established March 2006), Jason's commitment to researching, investigating and the search to explain the paranormal continues. You can find out more about Jason at his Official website (www.jasonday.co.uk).

A Brief History of Chelmsford

Chelmsford is located in the county of Essex, within the London commuter belt, approximately thirty-two miles north-east of Charing Cross, London.

There have been settlements in Chelmsford since ancient times. Evidence of a Neolithic and a late Bronze Age settlement have been found in the Springfield suburb, dating occupancy as far back as 3000 BC.

Later, a Roman fort was built in the area in AD 60, and a civilian town grew up around it. The town was given the name of Caesaromagus (the market place of Caesar), although the reason for it being given the great honour of bearing the imperial prefix is unclear. Possibly Caesaromagus was a failed 'planned town' provincial capital to replace Londinium or Camulodunum. The remains of a mansio, a combination post office, civic centre and hotel, lie beneath the streets of the modern suburb of Moulsham in Chelmsford, and the ruins of an octagonal temple are located beneath the Odeon roundabout.

An important Anglo-Saxon burial was discovered at Broomfield, to the north of Chelmsford, in the late nineteenth century and the finds are now in the British Museum. The road 'Saxon Way' now marks the site.

The town's current name is derived from 'Ceolmaer's ford' which was close to the site of the present High Street stone bridge. In the Domesday Book of 1086 the town was called 'Celmeresfort' and by 1189 it had changed to 'Chelmsford'. By 1199, the Bishop of London was granted a Royal Charter for Chelmsford to hold a market, marking the origin of the modern town.

Chelmsford became the seat of the local assize during the early thirteenth century (though assizes were also held at Brentwood) and by 1218 was recognised as the county town of Essex; a position it has retained to the present day. Chelmsford was significantly involved in the Peasants' Revolt of 1381, and Richard II moved on to the town after quelling the rebellion in London. *The Sleepers and The Shadows*, written by the late Hilda Grieve in 1988 using original sources, states:

> For nearly a week, from Monday 1 July to Saturday 6 July [1381], Chelmsford became the seat of government. The King probably lodged at his nearby manor house at Writtle. He was attended by his council, headed by the temporary Chancellor, the new chief justice, and the royal chancery.

Their formidable task in Chelmsford was to draft, engross, date, seal and despatch by messengers riding to the farthest corners of the realm, the daily batches of commissions, mandates, letters, orders and proclamations issued by the government not only to speed the process of pacification of the kingdom, but to conduct much ordinary day to day business of the Crown and Government.

Richard II famously revoked the charters which he had made in concession to the peasants on 2 July 1381, whilst in Chelmsford. It could be said that given this movement of government power, Chelmsford for a few days at least became the capital of England. Many of the ringleaders of the revolt were executed on the gallows at what is now Primrose Hill.

During Tudor times, Henry VIII purchased the Boleyn estate just to the North of Chelmsford. In 1516, he built Beaulieu Palace on the current site of New Hall School. This later became the residence of his then mistress, and later wife, Ann Boleyn. The palace went on to become the residence of Henry's daughter, by his first marriage; Mary I. During the 1700s the palace was demolished and rebuilt and in 1798 the English nuns of the Order of the Holy Sepulchre acquired the estate and opened a catholic school there the following year.

Another notable period in Chelmsford's history occurred during the 'Essex Witch Trials' of the seventeenth century. Many of the victims of Matthew Hopkins (the self-styled 'Witchfinder General') spent

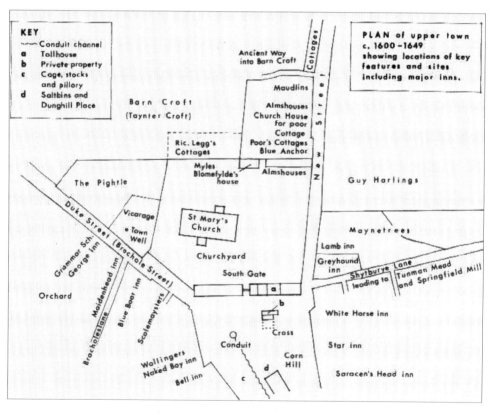

Map of Upper Chelmsford, 1600–1649.

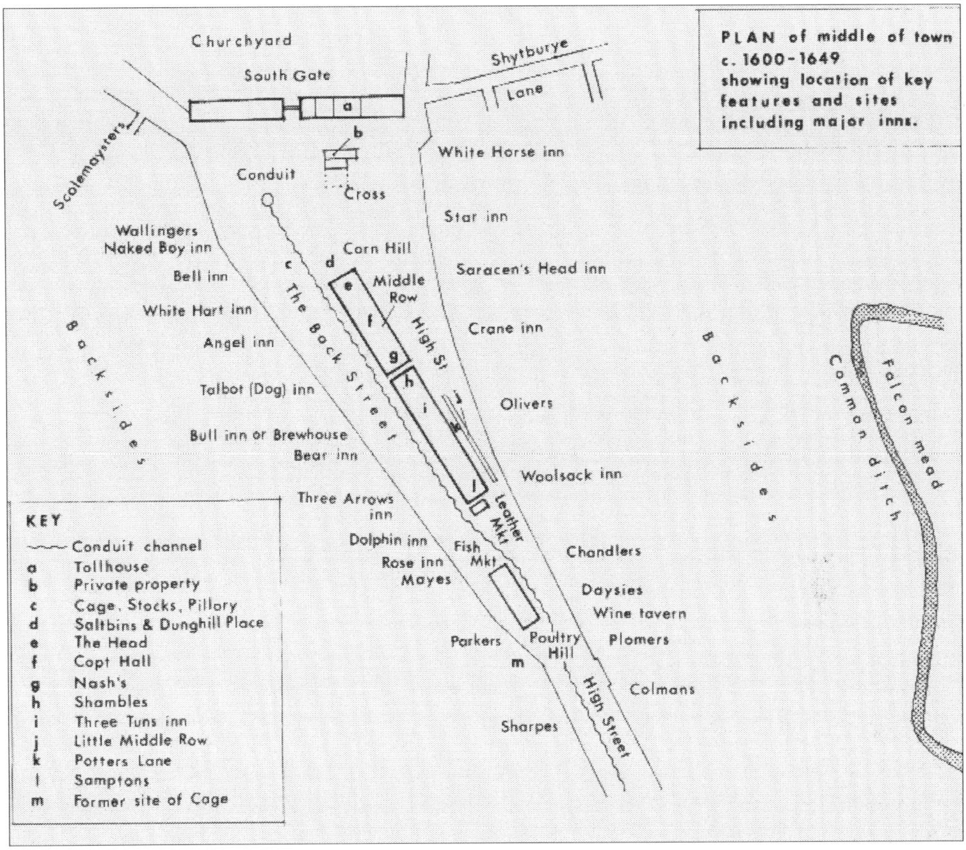
PLAN of middle of town
c. 1600-1649
showing location of key
features and sites
including major inns.
Churchyard
South Gate
Shytburye
Lane
Scolemaysters
Conduit
Cross
White Horse inn
Star inn
Wallingers
Naked Boy inn
Corn Hill
Bell inn
Middle Row
Saracen's Head inn
White Hart inn
The Back Street
High St
Crane inn
Angel inn
Backsides
Talbot (Dog) inn
Olivers
Bull inn or Brewhouse
Bear inn
Woolsack inn
Three Arrows inn
Leather Mkt
Dolphin inn
Fish Mkt
Rose inn
Mayes
Chandlers
Daysies
Wine tavern
Parkers
Poultry Hill
Plomers
Colmans
Sharpes
High Street
Falcon mead
Common ditch
KEY
Conduit channel
a Tollhouse
b Private property
c Cage, Stocks, Pillory
d Saltbins & Dunghill Place
e The Head
f Copt Hall
g Nash's
h Shambles
i Three Tuns inn
j Little Middle Row
k Potters Lane
l Samptons
m Former site of Cage

Map of Lower Chelmsford, 1600–1649.

their last days imprisoned in Chelmsford, before being tried at the Assizes and hanged for witchcraft: several of these executions taking place in the town itself.

During the Second World War, Chelmsford, an important centre of light engineering production, was attacked from the air on several occasions, both by aircraft of the Luftwaffe and by missile. The worst single loss of life took place on Tuesday 19 December 1944, when the 367th V2 rocket to hit England fell on a residential street in the town. The bomb hit Henry Road near Hoffman's ball bearing factory and not far from the Marconi Wireless Telegraph Company factory in New Street (which may also have been its intended target). Thirty-nine people were killed and 138 injured (forty-seven seriously). Several dwellings in Henry Road were completely destroyed, and many in nearby streets were badly damaged. A recently restored monument to the dead is in the borough cemetery in Writtle Road.

The GHQ Line was a defence line built in the United Kingdom during the Second World War to contain an expected German invasion. The British Army had abandoned most of its equipment in France after the Dunkirk evacuation. It was therefore decided to build a static system of defensive lines around Britain, all designed to compartmentalise the country and delay the Germans long enough for more mobile

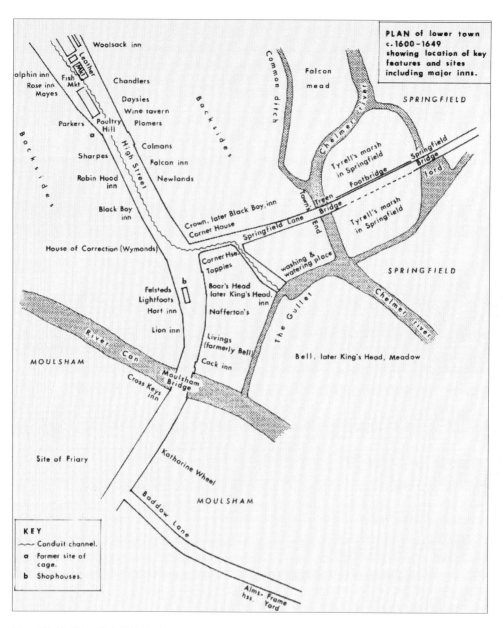

Map of Middle Chelmsford, 1600–1649.

forces to counter-attack. Over fifty defensive lines were constructed around Britain, the GHQ Line being the longest and most important, designed to protect London and the industrial heart of Britain. The line ran directly through Chelmsford and along this section the defences were made up of around 400 FW3 type concrete pillboxes (military bunkers), which were part of the British hardened field defences of the Second World War. Many of these pillboxes are still in existence to the north and south of the town. Faded camouflage paint still remains on old buildings near Waterhouse Lane.

Another location in Chelmsford that has significance to the Second World War is Hylands Park, the site of the annual V festival. During the war, Hylands Park hosted a Prisoner of War camp and a wireless command post for the 6th Anti-Aircraft Division.

Since the 1980s, Chelmsford has suffered from a decline in its defence-related industries, most notably The Marconi Company with all of its factories closing. There was an attempted regeneration during this decade with the construction of the Chelmer Village housing development, although the boost was short lived as the one-time largest employer in Chelmsford, R.H.P. (the former Hoffman ball bearing manufacturing company) closed its New Street/Rectory Lane site in 1989.

However, as Chelmsford moved into the new millennium it was not all doom and gloom. The town's location, close to London and at the centre of Essex, helped it grow in importance as an administrative and distribution centre. Some of the former R.H.P. factory remains and has been converted into luxury apartments and a health club and there have been large scale housing developments in the town, such as Beaulieu Park, 'The Village' and Chancellor Park.

The town currently has a population of approximately 157,500 which does not

The Marconi Statue in the Civic Theatre car park, Chelmsford. (Photograph by Jason Day)

include its 'other' residents – the ones from 'the other side'. Being located in one of the countries most haunted counties, Essex, it will come as no surprise that Chelmsford has a very rich haunted history of its own. Add to that the paranormal activity in the surrounding area and it could be that the Chelmsford area itself may be responsible for many of the hauntings attributing to the county's paranormal reputation.

One
The Ghosts
of Chelmsford

Spooks on Stage – Civic Theatre, Fairfield Road, Chelmsford

The Civic Theatre in Chelmsford, like many others around the country, is said to be haunted. Visitors often ask members of staff about the friendly man who has helped them find their seat or directed them to the toilets. A chill comes over them when they are told that he is one of the buildings many ghosts. The considerate phantom is believed to be the spirit of a technician who was killed on nearby Duke Street.

Spirits are said to tread the boards at Chelmsford Civic Theatre. (Photograph by Jason Day)

Other paranormal activity reported in the theatre includes disembodied footsteps on the stage and an overwhelming feeling of unease on the balcony and the stairs leading to the wardrobe and front of house office. Another apparition that frequents the building manifests itself in the form of a white butterfly. This spirit is traditionally seen every December during a show being staged in the week over the Christmas period.

The Figure In The Woods – Hylands Park, Chelmsford

In the early 1700s, a local and well respected lawyer, Sir John Comyns, purchased the manor of Shaxstones in Writtle, and commissioned the construction of a new family home on the estate, suitable for a man of his standing. Completed in 1730, Hylands House was an elegant two-storey red brick building in the Queen Anne style of architecture. The grounds were set out in the formal geometric style fashionable at the time, with a pleasure garden and small kitchen garden to the north of the house.

During the war, Hylands Park hosted a Prisoner of War camp and a wireless command post for the 6th Anti-Aircraft Division.

In 1944, the newly formed SAS (Special Air Services) used Hylands House as their Headquarters. Mrs Hanbury (the owner of the house) cheerfully accepted their presence and was regularly invited to dine in the Officers' Mess. On one memorable occasion, Captain Paddy Blair Maine (who went on to become this country's most decorated soldier) attempted to drive a Jeep up the grand staircase for a bet. The incident caused much commotion and Christine Hanbury dispatched the men to bed with instructions to remove the Jeep in the morning when they had clearer heads. The Jeep had to be dismantled before it could be removed.

To date, Hylands has had nine private owners, before the building and estate were finally bought by Chelmsford Borough Council in 1966.

There have been several accounts of alleged paranormal activity within the grounds of Hylands but one of the most intriguing stories has to be that which was the basis for the 2007 Greenway Entertainment movie; *Time of Her Life*. The creator of the film, Steven M. Smith claimed that the inspiration for the movie came from a meeting with an old friend in Chelmsford. Steven said his friend told him about a university student and two friends who were visiting Hylands Park one evening. The student claimed to have seen a shadowy figure of a man in a wooded area of the grounds that evening and was so disturbed by it that she

The impressive Hylands House, Chelmsford. (Photograph by Jason Day)

Hylands Park. (Photograph by Jason Day)

went into hiding. The friends had been filming their visit that night and also took some photographs. Steven tracked down one of the student's friends who had been present that night. The friend said they had not seen the apparition them self and that the video footage they had captured did not show any evidence of the figure either. The university student herself claimed to have photographic evidence of the ghost and also claimed that the spirit is now following her.

The validity of this story is open to question, as is the case in most alleged hauntings where there is no actual solid evidence. The fact remains, however, that this is one of many eyewitness accounts of paranormal phenomena within the grounds of Hylands House over a vast period of time. Surely, all of these witnesses can't be mistaken.

Spirits in the Attic – BBC Essex, New London Road, Chelmsford

The studios of radio station BBC Essex are situated within the former post office building on the corner of New London Road in Chelmsford. The white building is reputed to have been haunted by not one but several spirits, with visitors and staff reporting assorted paranormal phenomena over the years.

A paranormal investigation was carried out in the attic of the location in the late 1990s which yielded some rather interesting results. As related to me by staff at BBC Essex, paranormal investigators and mediums present claimed to have found evidence for at least five spirits being present in the building. Their findings concluded that an

Several spirits are said to haunt the studios of BBC Essex. (Photograph by Jason Day)

old lady, an angry old man, a nine-year-old girl and a boy and a girl in their teens all reside within the facility.

Further information garnered from the investigation through spirit communication revealed that the ghost of the nine-year-old girl is a happy little soul who craves attention. The story of the teenaged girl is, according to the team's findings, a far sadder one. The girl, named Amy, allegedly killed herself by jumping from one of the windows in the building. Amy had reportedly been raped and became pregnant. Unable to cope with her ordeal anymore she sadly took her own life. The angry old man who haunts the building is said to have been Amy's attacker.

The group also identified the ghost of the young boy as being a fifteen-year-old named Tom. Whether or not these spirits have moved on or still remain at the BBC Essex studios remains to be seen. Through further investigation and research perhaps

we may find out more about these poor souls and why they remain there.

The Caped Man – Patching Hall Lane, Chelmsford

During the 1970s, a group of teenagers were walking along Patching Hall Lane in Chelmsford. They noticed a figure further along the road and carried on walking. As they got closer they became more and more suspicious of the man.

One of the witnesses recalled the figure was tall and very pale, to the extent that he looked ill. He was also unusually dressed for the time, wearing a cloak and top hat. The group became so disturbed by the man that they turned around and ran away.

It was only when they looked back to see if the figure was following them that they realised he was not of this world. He had vanished before their eyes.

The caped entity of Patching Hall Lane. (Illustration by Tracie Wayling)

The Ghost Of Chelmsford Station – Chelmsford Railway Station, Railway Street, Chelmsford

In 1995, Mick Cash was working for a plumbing and heating company in Boreham, Essex. During his time working for this company he was given a job at Chelmsford railway station. He had not worked at the station before and all he knew about the job was that a faulty hot water cylinder had to be replaced.

On the first day of the job Mick was directed to a cafeteria on one of the station's platforms. One of the cafeteria's employees accompanied him down two floors, eventually reaching a corridor. The corridor turned back on itself and at the end of the corridor there was a door to a storeroom directly ahead and a door to the right which lead into the room where the faulty cylinder was situated. Upon inspecting the cylinder Mick realised he had a couple of days work ahead of him.

The room wasn't very big, twelve feet square perhaps; the cylinder that needed to be replaced was in the left-hand corner by the door. The only other objects in the room were an old, solid table with thick round turned legs and four chairs turned upside down resting on the table top. Mick Recalls: 'It was certainly one of the quietest places I had worked in, every time I put a tool down on the concrete floor the sound seemed exaggerated, I remember being very aware of my own breathing. It was quite unnerving at times.'

The first day's work was uneventful. However, as the job neared completion things were about to change. Mick describes the incident:

Late during the second day whilst working on pipe work on the new cylinder there was a horrendous crashing sound from behind me. I turned around and saw the table behind me sitting up on one of its sides and the four chairs falling about on the floor. I looked out of the door to see if perhaps one of our other plumbers had done it for a bit of a laugh but there was no one there, I was on my own. I must admit that it did scare the hell out of me and I told my boss that I wouldn't go back down there unless someone else from the company came down with me. Another plumber was sent

out to help me finish the job and there were no more incidents.

When the work had been completed, Mick wondered how he was going to get the old cylinder out of the station as it was a large galvanised steel type. He had seen a pair of doors along the corridor where it bent back on itself, but hadn't taken much notice of them. When Mick and his colleague opened them, they were very surprised to find out that they were at street level. Mick thought he had been working below ground level, though he recalled having to go below into a room accessed by an old hand made ladder. In this room there were no lights which would enable him to turn the power on to the cylinder electrics. He found this room very uncomfortable, particularly after his earlier

Chelmsford railway station, scene of poltergeist activity in 1995. (Courtesy of Wikimedia Comfmons)

experience. Mick finished the job without any further incident, but the unexplained phenomena he had witnessed has stayed with him to this day. As Mick explains:

> At the beginning of the job, when I was being taken down by the woman from the cafeteria, she told me that she thought the area was haunted and that there had been many unexplained incidents in the store-room next to where I was to be working, I thought she was just trying to unnerve me, it turned out I was wrong. Many times since this incident I have wondered what had occupied the site before the station had been built. The end wall of the room I had worked in had the top of what looked like a reasonable size arch, as if the floor I was working on had been built above an older structure, I never did try to find out more about the site.

Perhaps it was a spirit from the past that Mick had encountered that day.

The Trapped Souls – Chelmsford Prison, Springfield Road, Chelmsford

The first brick that began the life of Chelmsford prison was laid in 1822. The prison was opened as a county gaol eight years later in 1830. During its chequered history, the prison expanded in 1996 and has gone on to become a Category B prison and young offender's institute.

Over the years, the prison has also been in the public spotlight following its use as a location for the media in both the television and music industries. In 1979, the BBC filmed a feature length special of the television comedy show *Porridge* entirely on location at the prison. The recording of a live music album also took place at the facility when punk rock band The Sex Pistols recorded their album *Live at Chelmsford Top Security Prison* there.

In addition, the prison has seen its share of negative publicity too. In 1999, the management at Chelmsford Prison were severely criticised by the Chief Inspector of Prisons, after findings that staff were failing to respond to cell alarms, five years after a prisoner was beaten to death by his cell-mate. The prison was also criticised for unacceptably bad conditions of clean-liness. A further inspection a year later confirmed these failings. By 2002 reports cited that, 'conditions at Chelmsford [were] condemned as "poor and cramped" by the gaol's board of visitors.'

However, in 2005, Chelmsford was commended following an inspection for improving standards and procedures for inmates at the prison. This was con-firmed a year later by the Independent Monitoring Board which praised the new management at the prison. Presently Chelmsford Prison accepts adult male prisoners and young offenders, convicted or on remand direct from courts within its local catchment area.

Many paranormal investigators and researchers believe that there are certain conditions that create the right atmos-phere in which a haunting can manifest itself. Some believe that a building that has been the location of an event, or events, of great happiness or grave sadness is an ideal place for a haunting to occur. The theory behind this is that the energy created by such events is used to somehow 'burn' the images of it into the fabric of the building and, when the conditions are right, play the event back like a recording. This is what is known as a residual haunting. These same energies are also said to feed the spirits that are grounded on the earth at present. These spirits use the energy to manifest themselves. Unlike with a residual haunting, it is believed that spirits that are grounded are able to interact with those that witness their manifestation. With nearly 200 years of history, Chelmsford prison is such a place. Inside its walls there has been much sorrow, misery, agony and death, all of which, some would have us believe, would create the perfect conditions in which a haunting could occur. It seems in this instance this would appear to be the case.

Obviously, a working prison would be impossible to investigate for a team of ghost hunters or a paranormal investigator but there have been several eyewitness reports of paranormal activity that have been documented at Chelmsford prison over the years. Colin Brown has collated dozens of accounts from both members of staff and inmates themselves who have experienced the unexplained within the buildings walls.

Some years ago, a Principal Officer at the prison was in the reception area when he realised it was time for him to make his way to another part of the building for the 8.30 p.m. roll call. He walked along the passage from reception and reached the double gates to the inner forecourt. At this point, the officer saw a woman who he thought he recognised from her hairstyle. He assumed that it was one of his female colleagues, who was due to work the night shift at the prison that evening. As he approached her he commented that she had arrived rather early for work, he then stopped dead in his tracks as he realised the woman was not who he had first thought she was. The woman was wearing a crinoline dress and a bonnet and after gazing at her for a couple of seconds she disappeared. The officer continued on to the centre where another colleague commented on how pale his complexion looked. The officer who had witnessed the ghostly woman in the bonnet commented later that the experience had not frightened him, it was just completely unexpected.

The same apparition has been seen on several occasions and quite recently, according to other reports from within the prison. Between 2007 and 2008 Officer LC was working a night shift on B Wing. LC was sitting in an outer office that has a glazed wall which looks onto the landing. As the shift went on, LC had the feeling that somebody was watching him so he looked up, at which point he was confronted by a straight-faced woman staring at him through the window. LC described the woman as being upright against the glass and wearing a dress with a ruffled collar; although the figure was more of a shadow than a person he could definitely see by its outline that it was a female. LC wondered whether the figure could just be a reflection so he looked away to re-focus his eyes and then looked back at the window. The woman had disappeared. The next report of the ghostly lady followed a year later. In 2009, Officer TB reported seeing a pair of female legs on the stairs that lead in-between landings on G Wing. This sighting, although most likely paranormal, cannot definitely be attributed to the same apparition as the witness only saw the figure from the knees down. One of the most recent reports of the ghostly lady came in July 2011 from an officer who was working on A Wing. Officer MP was on the second landing of the wing when he noticed something rather peculiar on the landing below him. MP saw the 'frosted image' of a woman walking out of the servery and along the landing. He observed her for a few seconds before she disappeared. According to the witness the woman was wearing a crinoline dress, very much like the apparition that had been reported before.

Another prevalent phantom at Chelmsford Prison may also be from a similar era. Whilst sitting in the staff room on F Wing one evening, Prison Officer CS saw somebody pass the window from the corner of his eye. A fellow officer was also present at the time and also saw the figure that was carrying a lamp. Both men were so convinced that they had seen somebody on the landing that they called the police in to check.

In 1996, Officer TW saw an old-fashioned prison warder walking from landing A1 to landing A2 of A Wing. TW described the figure as wearing an old belt and cap and carrying a lamp. The sighting occurred at around midnight and lasted for a few seconds. TW was walking towards the figure at the time but decided to make an abrupt u-turn and walk away.

The staff are not the only witnesses when it comes to the phantom prison warder that patrols the prison. A young prisoner that was housed in cell C3-28 reported seeing the shadow of a man in the corner of his cell holding a lantern and staring at him one evening. The description he gave matched that of a typical prison warder from the Victorian era. This testimony would also have had some substance provided to it by the history of the prison; in 1845 the goal underwent a building program that involved enlarging the cells. This was achieved by knocking through the front walls of the cells and incorporating a portion of the original corridor into each one. The part of the cell that the witness attested to seeing the ghostly warder in would have originally

A spectral warder walks the corridors of Chelmsford Prison. (Illustration by Jason Day)

been the corridor outside the cell and would have been where the warder stood to check on the inmates occupying the cell.

Many would think that having two resident ghosts is more than enough; however, several other apparitions have been seen within the prison. The prison staff room is located in what used to be the old Chapel of the prison. Whilst heading into the staff room to have his tea one afternoon Officer LC received an unexpected surprise. At around 5.45 p.m. LC opened the door to the staff room and upon entering saw a figure dressed in priest's robes heading into the kitchen.

Another strange figure was seen during a night shift by Officer JM. During the shift, JM was stood beside a vending machine when somebody walked by. The figure was only visible from the waist up and JM recalled seeing the form of a body, shoulders, head and a hat. JM's back suddenly went cold as the male figure strode purposefully by, looking over his shoulder. Not long afterwards JM recalled the details of the encounter to a female officer. She replied 'Wait until you smell him. That'll really freak you out.' Apparently the female officer had also encountered the spirit, who she described as smelling of a particular brand of aftershave.

During a night shift Officer PH was alone on A Wing. The area was secured and not even other staff members had access to the area. During the shift, the officer was sitting in the office using a computer and from the corner of his eye he observed a figure run past the door. He leapt from his chair and drew his stave, running onto the landing. After a thorough search PH realised that there was nobody there.

During an afternoon shift in the Performance Management department of the prison, in the early 2000s, another illusive spirit was seen. Officer MS was seated at his desk on the second floor of the old hospital when he saw a figure swing around the door frame to a back storage room. It was as if the figure was looking to see who was in the room. MS commented to his colleague, Senior Officer GB, who was also in the room at the time, that he did not realise their co-worker MH was still at work, as she usually finished her shift at lunchtime. GB replied that MH was not at work and that she had indeed gone home. Officer PH checked the room that the figure had appeared from and it was empty. PH mentioned the occurrence to his boss and they left to go home. On the way out they passed beneath a locked hatch in the ceiling that gives access to the roof space. Both men heard a series of unexplained bangs through the hatch as they left.

One mysterious figure that several witnesses attest to having encountered could very well have been responsible for many of the 'corner of the eye' sightings at the prison. This entity is usually described as a shadow. On one occasion, Officer MP saw the shadowy figure on the stairs at the back of E Wing offices, whilst Officer TW saw the same entity looking into a cell on E Wing at a different time. The officer assumed it was a nurse and went to say hello. As he approached to greet the figure it disappeared. The same officer was on the ground floor of the Old Hospital, accompanying a prisoner, when they both saw a shadow move from the stairs to the finance office.

Along with the visual reports of apparition sightings at Chelmsford Prison there is also a vast amount of physical paranormal activity reported. Objects are said to be displaced and staff have even been known to have been pushed, suggesting that there may also be poltergeist activity within the building. At 3 a.m. one day, Officer LC was making a visit to a fellow officer who was working in security, which was located on the first floor of the Old Hospital. LC was wearing a backpack and carrying mail. He finished his visit and began descending the stairs, as he reached halfway he felt himself forced back against the wall. It was not until he reached the ground floor that the oppressive force dissipated. Other reports tell of bins being found in the middle of E Wing landing, although there were no other members of staff on the landing and all of the prisoners were locked in their cells, and a plastic cup being kicked at an Officer in the Health Care Centre at 3 a.m. by an unseen entity. In 1982, Officer DK and his colleague DH were working in the prison hospital on a night shift. They went upstairs to look for a deceased prisoner's file and discovered it was not in the filing cabinet where it should have been. They found it on the bottom shelf and as Officer DH placed a hand on it to pick it up they heard the distinct click of the metal light switch and the light turned off. Officer DK went to switch the light back on and nothing happened. The two officers looked at each other and made a hasty retreat back downstairs. As they got halfway down the stairs the light over the stairs went out and the officers remained in their office for the rest of the shift, waiting to be relieved. The first person to arrive for the day shift was the Hospital Principle Officer who exclaimed to DH and DK, 'Why are all the lights on?' An even more alarming example of physical paranormal activity occurred when Officer TW was stood at the corner of the first landing of C Wing one day. Out of the blue, vicious banging began emanating from the closed cell next to him; he reported that it was as if somebody was kicking the door from the inside. Upon inspection he discovered the cell was empty.

Amongst Colin Brown's collated reports from the prison are numerous instances of audio phenomena that range from footsteps and bangs, to whistles and voices. At half past seven one evening, Officer TB reported hearing a whistling on G Wing. He recalled that it was not the tuneful whistling of a song but more like that of somebody whistling to get somebody's attention. The officer's first thought was that it was a prisoner on the landing who was out of his cell. As G Wing was on patrol state at the time, all prisoners were supposed to be in their cells so he searched the landings. TB could find nobody else on the landings, even after searching cupboards for rouge prisoners: he never found the source. Officer DK joined Chelmsford Prison in 1980 and recalled spending most of his early days there working nights in the hospital. He would often hear banging noises from upstairs at around 3 a.m., even though the new hospital area was yet to begin admitting prisoners. Footsteps are commonly heard along the landings throughout the prison, even when there is nobody around. A typical example of this being: one morning at around three when Officer TW was patrolling behind the kitchen area he heard footsteps in the gravel following behind him, only to look around and discover he was alone.

One of the most interesting, and slightly disturbing, cases of audio phenomena at the prison occurred between July and August 2011. At around 4.45 p.m. Officer IB was entering the corridor at the back of the Healthcare Centre of the prison. The Officer was supposed to collect somebody from the centre but it transpired that they were no longer there. As IB passed the door to the Day Care Centre, which is on the ground floor to the Health Care Centre, an angry voice shouted from within the room. The voice exclaimed, 'F'ing let me out of here. It's dark in here!' At the time nobody should have been in the room so IB investigated. As soon as he opened the door to the Day Care Centre the obscenities ceased. After looking around he discovered nobody was there.

The most frequently encountered audio phenomena within the building is also a very unexpected one. The sound of children playing is an all too frequent sound around the prison. Whilst unlocking cells one morning, Officer SH heard the sound of children running around B Wing landing. He recalled the sound of children giggling, running, then stopping and then running again. They seemed to be playing a game although they were nowhere to be seen. On another occasion a prisoner on B Wing asked an officer why there were children playing outside his cell. Officer LC

also reported hearing the sound of children laughing during a shift at the prison. He said that the sound echoed from the end of three landings whilst he was on B or C Wing.

LC thought the noise may have been a television that a prisoner had turned up, but as he stepped onto the landing to tell the prisoner to turn his television down the voices stopped. Officer JM also encountered the ghostly children on C Wing. During a night shift his combat belt came undone for no apparent reason, he then heard the sound of two girls at the far end of the landing. It sounded to him that they had stopped what they were doing, laughed and ran skipping towards him. He assumed the ghostly children had played a prank on him. A senior officer reported that the yards patrol on night shift had a room under a croft, opposite the POA Office. One night,

Ghostly Victorian children are often heard within the confines of Chelmsford Prison. (Illustration by Jason Day)

in that room, the officer distinctly heard the sound of children crying. A further report from between July and August 2011 states that a prisoner who was in the Health Care Centre asked the staff there why there were young girls running around the exercise yard laughing and joking.

As with the Victorian prison warder, there is historical evidence to explain as to why there may be the spirits of children within the walls of Chelmsford Prison. During the mid 1800s it was a requirement that the governor of a prison live within the four walls of the gaol. The second governor of what is now Chelmsford Prison, Captain Henry McGorrey and his family did just that. In August 1862, his seven-year-old son William was struck down with Diphtheria and died. Just eight days later Captain McGorrey's twelve-year-old daughter Ann also died. The remainder of the McGorrey family moved out whilst the house was given a deep clean. They moved back into the house in the autumn of the same year and soon afterwards a third child, five-year-old Mary Ann McGorrey (named after her mother) died; this time of scarlet fever. It was considered too dangerous for the family to live inside the gaol anymore and the family moved into a new house, which was built just outside the perimeter wall. Unfortunately, McGorrey's wife, Mary Ann, died soon after in 1868 and his other ten-year-old daughter died just three years later. McGorrey himself died in 1893, at the age of eighty. The family are all buried in Springfield Holy Trinity churchyard, which is situated adjacent to the prison wall. Perhaps, then, the phantom children that currently reside within the prison are William, Ann, Mary Ann and Florence. This information may also lead us to the identity of the ghostly lady that is often seen. It could be quite possible that she is Mary Ann McGorrey, searching for her children. Some researchers also believe that the identity of one of the ghosts of Chelmsford Prison may in fact be William Calcraft, the most famous English hangman of the nineteenth century, who carried out many an execution at the prison.

There is no doubt that there are an abundance of witnesses to the hauntings at Chelmsford Prison, but what of the hard evidence? WF, who monitored CCTV at the establishment, reported seeing orbs 'dance all night' around a prisoner he was monitoring in the Health Care Centre. Another CCTV operator, JA, also reported seeing orbs around the prisoners that were under constant supervision in the Health Care Centre. JA also recalled that during one instance when he was making fun of one of the patients an orb turned and flew at the surveillance camera. JW then felt a rush of wind pass through the office where he was watching the CCTV monitors. Officer LC was working a night shift on E Wing, sitting in the centre bubble watching the CCTV monitors. At around 11 p.m. he saw a man walking up the left hand side of the stairs from the first to the second floor on the CCTV screens. The description LC gave of the man was that he was dressed in prison clothing (a pale blue t-shirt) and suffered from male pattern baldness. Upon investigation nobody was missing from their cells and unfortunately the CCTV had not recorded the incident.

Probably the most dramatic incident of paranormal activity reported from the prison comes from Officer SH. During his time at the prison an inmate living in cell B3-24 had made repeated requests to move cell. One day, when his cell was unlocked the prisoner emerged from his cell shaking and very traumatised maintaining that there was something in the room. He had been the only person in the cell. Officer SH went to open the cell door but it would not move. He finally managed to push the door open but it had felt like somebody had put their hands on his chest and was pushing against him, such was the resistance. It was thirty degrees Celsius on B Wing landing, but as SH entered the cell it was like walking into a freezer, after making sure nobody else was in there he left the cell. SH called out to another officer on the second landing and she came over. He asked her to go into the cell, which once again had the door closed. SH was sure he had left the door open when he came out of the cell and he had not heard the door slam shut. The female officer went to open the door and without prompting proclaimed, 'Something is wrong.' She opened the door and the cell, which had been freezing, was now the same temperature as the landing. The prison chaplain was later called and he performed an exorcism on the cell. The chaplain told SH that there was something wrong with the cell but it should be alright now.

I think we can safely say that Chelmsford Prison certainly has a case for being the most haunted place in Chelmsford.

The Box Monster – The Spotted Dog, Tindall Street, Chelmsford

In 1793, a Mr William Clakar sold an unnamed public house to Messrs Woodcock and Johnstone. The inn was situated in Chelmsford on Back Street, which became Conduit Street and was finally named Tindal Street. The pub became the Spotted Dog Inn and was run by Elizabeth Holmstead and then William Pearson. It was during this period that tragedy struck the establishment.

On the 22 October 1804, a troop of Hanoverian soldiers were staying at the Spotted Dog Inn. The pub was frequently used as a resting place for moving troops. On this occasion there were around 120 men staying at the Spotted Dog. Some of the troops stayed on the premises, with many more accommodated in the stables. During the night they were woken from their slumber to find that the stables were on fire. The alarm had been raised and the men frantically tried to escape the blaze but they were hampered in doing so as the only means of escape was a door which was closed from the outside. The men began to panic and did not realise that the door could be opened from the inside by putting a finger through a hole by the side of door, which would enable them to release the latch on the outside. Some of the soldiers were eventually saved but tragically thirteen of their comrades perished. The cause of the fire was believed to have been a cigarette igniting the straw that the men were sleeping on. A verdict of accidental death was returned and the soldiers were given a military funeral.

The Spotted Dog was soon open again and over the next century saw a myriad of landlords and landladies come and go. There were hushed rumours and whispered gossip that the building at 24 Tindal Street may be haunted, but it was not until the 1950s that there were reports that the rumours could be true.

A room in the inn was believed to be haunted by the spirit of a previous guest who had been murdered in his sleep. Paranormal activity escalated in the room to such an extent that the room was eventually sealed and never used again. The inn became infamous for its sealed room and the grisly history behind it.

Around twenty years later, the Spotted Dog Inn was demolished. Between 1969 and 1970 the entire left-hand side of Tindal Street (including the Spotted Dog) was flattened to make way for a new shopping centre. Eyewitness reports recount that an unseen entity is believed to haunt the shopping centre. Several shops have reported paranormal activity in their premises, including cardboard boxes being thrown around by an unseen force. Such is the extent of this phenomenon that the entity that is believed to be responsible has become referred to as 'The Box Monster'.

History would suggest that the identity of this spirit is probably one of two possibilities. Either he is one of the soldiers who were tragically killed in the fire at the Spotted Dog in 1804, or he is the ghost of the man who was murdered at the inn, finally freed from the sealed room to haunt the shopping centre when the building was demolished to make way for it.

The Restless Spirits – The Angel Inn, Main Road, Broomfield, Chelmsford

The Angel Inn on Main Road in Broomfield dates back to the fifteenth century. The building was originally a hall house with north and south wings, the columns of which are still supporting the roof some 600 years later. By 1702 the house had become an inn and served as a coaching house on the main road to and from Chelmsford. Over 300 years later it remains an inn to this day. There had been several reports of paranormal activity in the pub over the years and by the early 2000s many of the staff working there reported witnessing some paranormal phenomena for themselves.

In an endeavour to find the cause of this phenomena, many paranormal investigations have been conducted at the Inn over the years. These have involved both scientific and spiritual experiments during overnight vigils. Séances, Ouija boards and pendulums have been used along with night-vision cameras, EMF meters and laser thermometers. The results of the experiments and the vigils themselves have met with varying degrees of success.

The conclusions that have been drawn from the findings of the investigations are that several entities reside at the Inn, including a distressed spirit that refuses to leave. Who the spirits were at the Angel Inn is still unclear, maybe further investigation of the building may enable investigators to discover this and perhaps more.

A negative energy is believed to reside within the Angel Inn. (Photograph by Jason Day)

The Knocking Of the Dead – Well House, Broomfield, Chelmsford

The Well House was a building located on the outskirts of Broomfield in Chelmsford and received its name from the fact that it was supposed to have had a well beneath it. A widower named Thomas Dixon resided in the house in 1772 and was later joined by his son Robert (who was also a widower). The father and son lived at Well House for thirteen years until the Easter of 1785 when an ageing Thomas was taken ill. A doctor and nurse were called to the house and tended to Thomas during his illness. At around midnight on the Easter Monday the doctor and nurse were watching Thomas at his bedside when there was an abrupt knocking at the door. The nurse opened the door and found nobody there. She closed the door and returned to the bedside. Again there was knocking at the door and once more the nurse answered to find nobody there. No sooner had she returned to Thomas' bedside and the knocking began again. The irate doctor swore and the nurse once more opened the door. This time the nurse checked the whole area and could find nobody and no possible cause for the knocking. Shortly afterwards Thomas Dixon died. Within hours Thomas' son Robert had died too. A double funeral was held for father and son on the 10 April 1785 in Broomfield Cemetery.

No cause was ever found for the mysterious knocking that night but locals would later relate the story citing it as 'the knocking of the dead'.

Molly Ram – Molram's Lane and The Bringey, Great Baddow, Chelmsford

Molram's Lane in the Great Baddow area of Chelmsford is said to be haunted by the spirit of the person the road was named after; Molly Ram was murdered by her husband at the turn of the 1800s and her ghost has been seen walking along the lane on several occasions. An apparition witnessed in a nearby street called The Bringey is also believed to have been Molly.

The Monk and the Soldiers – St Mary's Church, Church Street, Great Baddow, Chelmsford

St Mary's Church in Great Baddow dates back several centuries. The towers and aisles of the building hail from the 1300s, with other parts of the church being restored between 1892 and 1903. There have been several sightings of phantoms both inside and outside the church and they have all been, to some extent, slightly bizarre.

At least one report recollects a group of ghostly Civil War soldiers grouped outside the church staring intently at the building. It is not known why the spectral military men were keeping such a close eye on the church or what their intentions were.

The other spirit witnessed at St Mary's is that of a monk. Legend has it that there were secret tunnels beneath the church and that a door on the west side of the building is connected to them. Perhaps this is why the monk has been seen making his way towards the door before disappearing. What is not so clear cut is why he appears to 'slide' down the aisles whilst heading towards the door.

In the past, an eerie spectral army have been seen within the grounds of St Mary's Church. (Photograph by Jason Day)

The Ghost of Thomas Kidderminster – The White Horse Inn, Great Baddow, Chelmsford

Modern reports of paranormal activity at the White Horse Inn in Chelmsford cite a spirit known as 'Albert' to be responsible, however, there are records of a haunting in the building that dates back to the 1600s and there is also a very dark story behind it.

Thomas Kidderminster was a self-made man from Ely in Cambridgeshire. Thomas became steward to the Bishop of Ely, bought land in the area and also began lending money to others. He later married and when he began suspecting that some of his debtors may become bad risks he decided to sell his properties in Ely, reclaim what debts he could and relocate. He sent his pregnant wife to London and told her he would follow in around ten days. After settling his business Thomas then changed up to £600 of silver for gold in Cambridge and set about his plans to travel to London.

Thomas began his journey in April 1654, and as the main path to London was a very dangerous road at the time he opted to take another route. Accompanied by a guide, Thomas chose to take the by-road through Chelmsford. Upon reaching the White Horse Inn he dismissed his guide and booked a room as he had done on several occasions before. Thomas Kidderminster was said to have left the inn and was never seen again.

Throughout the following years, Thomas' wife Anne continued to search for her husband. She followed up leads and reports that he had been seen in Amsterdam, Barbados and Ireland. None of these sightings led to the discovery of her missing husband. Nearly a decade passed and one day Anne Kidderminster was at home in her sister's company. Anne's sister was reading the *Publick Djurnal* newspaper when she suddenly spotted a very interesting article. According to the report the new owner of the White Horse Inn had decided to replace a fence between his property and that of his neighbour. The new owner, Mr Turner, had opted to replace the fence with a clay wall which required digging. As he set about his task he unearthed what he at first presumed to be a brown bowl. Upon further inspection it was discovered to be a human skull with an ominous hole in its left side. Further bones were unearthed and it was ascertained that the body of a man had been bent double and crammed into a makeshift grave on the grounds. With the former Innkeeper, Mr Sewell, having died of the plague before the discovery, his wife was questioned about the find. Her answers were inconclusive regarding the deceased and his identity, so the article asked for any information anybody may have regarding the matter. According to the report the remains may have laid in their grave for up to ten years, approximately the same period of time that Thomas Kidderminster had been missing. Anne's sister relayed the article to her, exclaiming there was news of Thomas, and Anne contacted the relevant person about her husband's disappearance.

Friends of Anne Kidderminster had previously tried to deter her from continuing her search for her missing husband, deeming that it may be a lost cause. It would appear that, from testimony of her own, Anne had on several occasions received visions of Thomas. Until now the visions had been of her husband, dressed in his usual attire, looking upon her very sternly as she lay in bed. Recently Anne had seen the vision of

Thomas dressed in a white sheet which had streaks of blood upon it. The visions, coupled with the recent information from the newspaper article, convinced Anne that the remains found at the White Horse Inn were indeed those of her husband. Anne now set about making her way to Chelmsford.

Anne reached Romford and it was here that a chance meeting with a stranger led to her garnering further information. Anne met a lady by the name of Mary Mattocks, who was visiting Romford on an errand. Mary was born and bred in Chelmsford and as a consequence was very knowledgeable about the town. When Anne asked Mary about Chelmsford and the White Horse, Mary had some rather interesting information for her. She told Anne that the present Innkeeper at the White Horse, Mr Turner, was a very good and honest man. The same could not be said for the previous owner, Mr Sewell. Mary believed that Mr Sewell ought to have been hanged as she alleged that there had certainly been a murder at the inn and that Mr Sewell was responsible. Mary even implicated the White Horse's ostler, Moses Drayne, as being an accomplice. Mary told Anne that Moses Drayne now lived in Romford, so Anne Kidderminster sent for him. Drayne found out what the purpose of Anne's meeting with him was and refused to come.

Anne then travelled the fifteen miles to Chelmsford and visited the White Horse Inn. Anne met with Mr Turner, the landlord, and explained that the remains found at the inn may be of her missing husband. Turner recounted the story of his discovery of the body and suggested that Anne should visit the former landlord's wife; together they set off for Mrs Sewell's house. Mrs Sewell was far from pleasant on their arrival and accused Mr Turner of causing trouble for her. When she found out who Anne Kidderminster was and the purpose of her visit she would say no more.

Anne stayed at the White Horse Inn that evening and encountered strange paranormal phenomena during the night. She stayed in the room adjacent to the one her husband had slept in and was so terrified at the prospect of staying overnight that she requested the maid slept in the same bed with her. Whilst in her room Anne heard a loud noise in the next room that echoed out into the gallery. Such was the violence of the noise that the whole room seemed to shake. Shortly afterwards, Anne saw the latch of her room door move up and down, she was so unnerved by the whole experience that she did not leave her bed until the morning.

The following day, Anne asked the maid if she had heard anything during the night to which she replied no. Anne explained what had happened to the landlord and he told her that such unexplained things had often been heard before at the inn.

Having had no success with Mrs Sewell, Anne once more turned her attention to Moses Drayne. She returned to Romford and eventually confronted Drayne in the One Bell Inn. Anne asked Drayne to describe the man who had left his horse at the inn and what he was wearing the night her husband disappeared. Drayne replied that the man was tall, big, and portly and had short brown hair. He also added that the man was wearing dark grey clothes and a black satin cap. The description fit that of Thomas Kidderminster perfectly, except he had worn a grey cap. When Anne mentioned the grey cap to Drayne his face became pale and he could no longer look her in the eye. Drayne told Anne that Mary Kendall was the maid at the White Horse at the time of her husband's disappearance and that she could probably tell her more.

During this time Mrs Sewell had died, but with momentum gathering a warrant for Moses Drayne's arrest was issued and (after going on the run) Mary Kendall was also arrested. Convinced that her running away would be seen as an admission of guilt, Mary Kendall decided to reveal the story of what had happened to Thomas Kidderminster that evening.

Firstly, Mary explained that she had ran away, as Mr and Mrs Sewell's daughters had threatened that if she told the story of what had happened they would swear against her and she would hang. Having given her explanation Mary now continued to tell her story of the night's events.

That evening, Mary was working as a maid at the White Horse Inn. She had gone to fetch a pair of bed sheets to make up the bed in the guest room known as the King's Arms. When she entered the bedchamber she noticed that Thomas Kidderminster was already in the room; he was stood with his back towards the fire, drinking beer with Mr and Mrs Sewell. Thomas asked Mary if she was the Sewell's daughter and she replied that she was the maid. As she prepared a napkin to make Thomas a sleeping cap Mary saw Thomas hand over a cloak bag to Mr Sewell for safekeeping. Thomas told Sewell that the bag contained nearly £600 and writings of considerable value, at this point Mrs Sewell told Mary to retire to bed. Mary was told not to go to her own bedchamber, but to retreat to a chamber at the end of the house, farthest from Thomas's room. After entering the bedchamber Mary was locked in the room by Mrs Sewell.

At around 2 a.m. Mary heard a noise that sounded like 'a great fall of something' that she said shook the whole house. It was not until the following morning that Mrs

The White Horse in Great Baddow, the scene of murder and hauntings. (Photograph by Jason Day)

Sewell unlocked the bedchamber door and Mary went downstairs. Mary found Mr and Mrs Sewell sat by the fire drinking merrily with Moses Drayne. The Sewell's two daughters were also present and none of them looked as though they had slept the previous evening. Later that morning Mary was aware that she had not seen Thomas Kidderminster. She asked Mrs Sewell if he had left the inn and she replied that he had. Mrs Sewell told Mary that Thomas had left her a groat and gave it to her. Mary said that she would go and clean the room that Thomas had stayed in and Mrs Sewell told her that wouldn't be necessary as she and her daughters had already done it.

The same morning two local women enquired at the inn about a commotion they had heard in the early hours of the morning. One woman was waiting for her husband to return home and the other had been passing the inn at around 2 a.m. to perform washing duties in the town. They both claimed to have heard a man's voice coming from the inn that shouted, 'What! Will you rob me of my money, and murder me too? If you take my money, spare my life.' They then heard a heavy fall and the sound of furniture being hurled around. The lights went out in the room and then all was quiet again. They were told that they must have been mistaken, as no noise came from the inn that night and that only the Sewell family had been present in the building that evening.

One Sunday morning, shortly afterwards, Mr Sewell gave Mary the key to his room and instructed her to fetch his cloak. Upon opening a chest in the chamber she discovered Thomas Kidderminster's suit of clothes and the cloak bag she had seen Thomas hand over to Mr Sewell.

The door to the room Thomas had stayed in remained locked for the next eight to nine weeks and nobody was permitted to enter it. Mary enquired as to why the room was not made available to guests as was usual, to which Mrs Sewell replied that the room was kept for gentlemen and thus far they had no guests fit to stay in it.

Eventually, Mary was sent to the room to fetch something. Mary took this opportunity to search the room and found Thomas Kidderminster's hat, boots, hanger and satin cap. She took the items downstairs where she confronted Mrs Sewell with the evidence. She questioned her as to whether Thomas Kidderminster had really left the inn that morning and gone to London. Moses Drayne, who was also present, called Mary a liar and claimed that the items were his. As they quarrelled Mrs Sewell attacked Mary, leaving her bloodied and dishevelled. Mary began shouting at Mrs Sewell, asking whether she intended to murder her as she had Thomas Kidderminster. It was at this point that Mr Sewell heard the commotion and entered the room. Mr Sewell persuaded Mary to hold her tongue and paid her £20 'hush money'. Moses Drayne, for his part was paid £60 and also took Thomas's clothes, which were sent to be dyed in Moulsham.

The Sewell's had been a poor family before the murder. Mary attested that following Thomas's disappearance they suddenly became quite wealthy. They bought and renovated a ruined malt house and were buying £40 worth of barley a day. It was also noticed that the Sewell's daughters were seen to be dressed in finery that they normally wouldn't have been able to afford.

Other evidence began to mount up against the Sewell's and Drayne; William Denton – Thomas Kidderminster's former servant – testified that the horse, clothes and hat had indeed belonged to his master.

A local farmer also came forward to testify

that he stayed overnight at the inn after selling barley. He had £20 on his person and, having heard the rumours about the murder, put furniture against his bedchamber door after he retired for the evening. During the night he heard Drayne and Mr Sewell come to the door and try the handle.

Following the trial, Mary Kendall was sent to prison for an indefinite period. The Sewell's daughters, Betty and Priss, were released as it was decided that there was not enough evidence to convict them. Mr and Mrs Sewell had both died before the trial and so could not be convicted. The final suspect, Moses Drayne, was sentenced to death for his part in the murder of Thomas Kidderminster and was hung.

From the historical evidence provided in this story it now becomes a bit of a dilemma as to who the ghost of the White Horse Inn could be. Could the spirit the staff have named 'Albert' in fact be somebody else?

Perhaps it is the evil landlord Sewell or his wife that haunts the building, looking for their next victim from beyond the grave. The ghostly footsteps heard coming from the attic stairs of the White Horse Inn could also be their equally despicable cohort Moses Drayne, or perhaps it may well be the poor spirit of Thomas Kidderminster, making himself known to those present in the building as he did to his wife over 350 years ago.

The Mysterious Case of E.P. – Dog and Gun Cottage, Great Leighs, Chelmsford

The Dog and Gun Pub was originally a coaching inn dating back to the 1700s. The pub is situated on Boreham Road on the outskirts of Chelmsford in Essex. Adjoined to the end of the pub are four cottages that were previously part of the inn itself. Apart from one or two further cottages on the quiet, country road there is little other civilisation around.

In 2006, a young couple had been living in one of the cottages that were attached to the pub, for roughly six months, and from day one they both had a deep nagging feeling that they were not the only ones in the building. For a fleeting second, the man of the house would often see a figure in the corner of the room, sometimes reflected in the living room mirror. His partner would also glimpse the figure occasionally, although not as often. She also found objects disappearing and reappearing regularly while at home by herself in the evening. Despite what some may think would be a natural reaction, the couple never felt unnerved by their experiences or scared of being alone in the house.

It was because of these experiences that they decided to invite Essex based paranormal group SPIRIT (Society for Paranormal Investigation, Research, Information & Truth) to investigate the property and, at the couple's request, try to communicate through an Ouija board. At the time, using this form of spirit communication was something the members of SPIRIT had never considered before, but as the couple were both very keen on this idea they accepted their invitation. The night of the investigation was the couple's last night in the cottage, most of their furniture and belongings had already gone to their new house.

At 9.15 p.m. on a very wet Saturday 6 May, the SPIRIT team arrived at the cottage and set up their equipment. They began conducting some baseline tests. Electro Magnetic Field (EMF) readings were of no use as throughout the cottage readings were too high due to electrical cables and wiring. When team member Alison White began taking temperature readings she had her first inkling that there may well be some unexplained energy within this ageing cottage. Team member and cameraman Simon Day was filming Alison taking the temperature readings, using night vision equipment in the upstairs bathroom. Gaining steady readings she was aware of a sudden temperature drop by a degree, simultaneous with Simon picking up an orb passing by her at waist height.

The scene in the lounge was now set to begin the Ouija board session. With the owners and two members of SPIRIT seated around the table they began. The participants each placed one finger on the glass and having cleared their minds they pictured passing a white energy around the circle. They said a spell to protect themselves and then called out, 'Is anybody here? We invite you to come and talk with us'. Nothing happened. A series of questions were asked and still no response. They spent forty-five minutes trying to communicate but nothing happened so they decided to take a break.

The Dog and Gun in Great Leighs has a long history of paranormal activity. (Photograph by Jason Day)

Above: Paranormal investigators were called to investigate this cottage at the Dog and Gun in 2006. (Photograph by Jason Day)

Left: SPIRIT paranormal investigator Simon Day prepares to investigate. (Photograph by Jason Day)

During the break, two team members went upstairs to take pictures of the bedroom and bathroom using their digital cameras. Having not picked up any alleged paranormal activity downstairs, and having no luck with the Ouija board, the decision was made to take the board upstairs to the bedroom. This decision turned out to be the best decision of the night.

Settling down on the floor, the owners of the cottage and SPIRIT team member Alison White surrounded the board and placed one finger each upon the glass; SPIRIT member Simon Day was filming events on camera and Jason Day was taking notes in the corner of the room. The moment the participants fingers touched the glass their questions were being answered on the board. Is there anybody there? Yes, came the reply.

Now, from here on in I leave you, the reader, to deduce what you will. Many believe that the Ouija board is not an accurate means of communicating with the spirit world and is open to fraud and misinterpretation. Others believe it to be a way of opening up a portal to communicate with the dead. That night, during the SPIRIT team's investigation, the glass glided over the board as if it were on ice.

When asked for a name the glass repeated itself, moving over to the letter E and then P, E and then P. Are these your initials? Yes. Are you male? No. Are you a female? Yes. As the questions were answered a profile of EP was beginning to form. EP alleged to have lived during the time of King George IV, living and working her entire life in Essex and never having ventured over the

The haunted bedroom in the Dog and Gun cottage. (Photograph by Jason Day)

borders. Residing at the cottage, which she explained was then one building connecting to the pub, she lived with her four children, and she also kept a horse and chickens. EP was thirty-eight when she died in the year 1828. She conveyed that if the team were to look in the graveyard at Great Leigh's church they would be able to see her grave. The male owner of the house asked if the figure he saw downstairs was EP. Yes, she replied. Have you moved things around downstairs, especially cigarette lighters? Yes. The conversation continued, after an hour the owner asked EP if she minded him leaving for a moment. The glass moved to No, the owner left the board and his partner and SPIRIT member Alison White carried on. With just the two of them they noted that the glass, while still moving, was not moving at the same pace with the same force, but on the owner's return to the board the glass pick up speed again. 'Do you need our energy to communicate?' they asked; yes was the reply. So it's easier with three people rather than two? Yes. Starting to feel weary, the participants around the Ouija board thanked EP for talking to them. Alison asked EP if she had heard the spell they said downstairs and if she would like them to say it again before they left. Yes she had and yes she wanted them to say it again. So they cast their spell of protection and ended the session.

The team were overwhelmed, at that moment they were convinced that they had just held a conversation with a dead woman, and if indeed they had, that would mean they must all now accept that they believed there is conscious life after death. As SPIRIT team member Alison White recalled:

It is hard to explain and if you have never experienced using an Ouija board it will be hard to believe, but I have complete faith that the three of us at the board that night were not consciously moving the glass. It is often said that it is the sub-conscious mind of the participants that move the glass, which up until this night I believed, but surely at some point we would have contradicted each other and the glass would then be pulled in separate directions. All I know is that there was no hesitation of the glass and each question was answered decisively.

The investigation ended at 2.10 a.m. on Sunday 7 May 2006 and the team left the location at 2.24 a.m.

Following the investigation, SPIRIT team member Alison went to the public record office and looked up burials at Great Leigh's in the year 1828. Nobody with the initials EP could be traced. The team also tried tracing the cottage back to the 1820s, again with no luck or sign of EP. The only information they could confirm was that it was King George on the throne when she died and throughout the majority of her life he was Prince Regent.

The Dog and Gun pub building itself had also seen paranormal activity in the past. During the 1944 case of the Scrapfaggot Green Poltergeist in Great Leighs, sceptical landlord Bob Reynolds, who had scoffed at reports of the paranormal activity in the village at the time, found a boulder the size of a beer barrel outside his pub door. Nobody knew how it had got there.

The Ghosts of the Inn – St Anne's Castle Inn, Great Leighs, Chelmsford

St Anne's Castle Inn in Great Leighs lays claim to being the oldest inn in England, and may possibly be the most haunted one too. The inn is mentioned in the Domesday Book of 1086, with others citing the inn's construction as being around 1170. The inn has certainly been around since the Middle Ages, with pilgrims making their way to Thomas A. Becket's tomb using the hostelry on route during the twelfth century. As time went on, the inn became a hermitage and also suffered a fire in the 1500s in which the original thatched roof was lost and replaced with tiles. There are, however, still remnants of the inns past remaining within the building, including timbers dating back hundreds of years and two tunnels in the cellar that reputedly linked the building with nearby Leez Priory and Great Leighs church. Amongst the famous visitors to the inn are reputed to be Queen Anne and the Little Leighs bodysnatcher Samuel Clark.

Recorded paranormal activity at the inn dates back as far as the late 1930s. During this period of time interest in the phenomena being experienced at the pub was so intense that the BBC broadcasted a program entitled *A Haunted House* from the building on April 15 1939. Five years later, the inn was again the subject of public interest when renowned ghost hunter Harry Price visited the establishment during his investigation of the Scrapfaggot Green Poltergeist in 1944. Harry met with landlord Alfred Sykes, who explained the nature of the haunting to him. Mr Sykes told Price that there was a bedroom in the inn that was considered so evil that nobody could sleep in it. Mr Sykes continued:

It is always like this. Nothing will stay put. Over and over again we have straightened up the place, only to find next morning that everything was higgledy-piggledy. We now use it as a lumber room, but boxes and furniture are scattered about night after night. No other part of the house is affected.

Price concluded that some of the alleged paranormal activity at St Anne's Castle Inn may very well have been genuine and following his investigation things escalated. Apparitions were sighted in the cellar by at least two witnesses and the lumber room was becoming so active that even pets were afraid to enter. Seventy-two years after the BBC broadcast from the inn, the haunted room was still having an effect on the residents and visitors of the pub. Those that have ventured into the room have claimed to have felt depressed and nauseous.

St Anne's Castle Inn, Great Leighs. (Photograph by Kelly Day)

43

The inn has a history dating back to the twelfth century. (Photograph by Kelly Day)

In 2011, landlady Pat Balcombe claimed that the room emanated such a bad feeling that she kept it bolted and only entered it when absolutely necessary.

Pat has also reported that poltergeist activity is still occurring in the pub during her residency there. She has witnessed the television turning itself on and off and CD's playing and stopping at will. Objects are said to disappear for a period of time, only to turn up again exactly where they had been left – a typical phenomena associated with a poltergeist infestation. These events have included two rather disturbing instances that could be put down to poltergeist activity.

The first example involved Pat's husband Dave. Dave prepares and cooks the food at the inn and is, to all intents and purposes, the pubs chef. As such, Dave takes his work very seriously and uses professional equipment, including a set of chef knives. One day, Dave was preparing some food when he noticed one of his knives was missing from the block he stood it in. He took particular notice of this as the knife in question had an orange handle and was one of his favourite knives to work with. Dave searched for the knife and asked other members of staff and family at the inn if they had seen it and everybody replied in the negative. Dave was rather annoyed and perplexed at the loss of the knife but as there was not a lot he could do about it he gave up on the search and continued his work.

A few weeks later, Dave was once again working in the kitchen, having pretty much forgotten about the missing knife. Whilst working away he put his hand into a container to reach for a spatula, not looking inside. He quickly retracted his hand and clasped it in pain as he realised he had cut himself. Dave looked inside the container and found to his astonishment that not only was his missing orange handled knife inside, but so were all of the other knives that were usually stood in the block. Even more alarmingly the knives were all sat with their blades pointing upwards. When asked, everybody who could have had any access to the kitchen and the knives denied any knowledge of how this happened.

The second instance of possible poltergeist activity was equally as alarming and

Members of staff have reported many unexplained incidents within the pub. (Photograph by Kelly Day)

even more dangerous. A fire broke out in the family bathroom and the emergency services were called in. Luckily, nobody was hurt and there was minimal damage. Upon investigation the cause was found to be the shower unit in the bathroom. The perplexing factor regarding the outbreak was that upon inspection the wiring behind the shower was found to be undamaged by the fire.

Other staff and customers have also encountered strange happenings at the inn, including the sighting of a ghostly cat and the unexplained smell of strong pipe smoke in the non-smoking bar.

In an attempt to discover who the ghosts of St Anne's Castle Inn are, there have been several paranormal investigations at the establishment. The findings of these investigations have been recorded and, where possible, attempts have been made to either verify or dispel the evidence.

Amongst the spirits said to reside at the inn are a small boy and a little girl. The children are said to play together but are only ever seen alone. The girl has long blonde curly hair and believed to have enjoyed helping in the kitchen during her lifetime, as she walks around the building with a mixing bowl. There are also said to be phantom monks and a spectral patron who sits in the bar smoking a pipe. The main bedroom is haunted by a lady named Elizabeth who walks around the room in her wedding dress and is often seen looking out of the window. It is believed that she is looking for her husband; perhaps he died or left her standing at the alter?

Two more spirits that some ghost hunters believe haunt the inn are slightly more unnerving. The first is the ghost of a man named George Harry Benfield. During a paranormal investigation at St Anne's, Benfield's spirit is believed to have made contact and imparted the following information. He lived at the nearby Old School House in Great Leighs with his family in the 1800s and was possibly a gunsmith. Benfield found out that his first born son was, in actuality, his brother's child and flew into a rage. Benfield attached a rope to a piece of wood, tied the rope around his wife and son's necks and turned it until the unfortunate mother and son's necks broke. Upon researching this information the paranormal investigators found that there was indeed a George Benfield who had been hung at Chelmsford in 1875 for killing his wife and son. The second spirit is believed to be that of an alleged local witch named Anne Huwghes who was executed in 1621.

Several mediums have visited the inn over the years and have also claimed to have communicated with the spirits there; some of which may have had even darker intents than George Benfield. Many have picked up on the presence of monks but have described their behaviour as anything but Christian. The phantom monks seem to be most active in the cellar. The cellar would have been the means by which the monks entered and left the inn, via the tunnels that were reputedly connected to Leez Priory. Whilst visiting the cellar one medium claimed she could 'feel darkness' and wanted to 'claw her way out' even though the cellar was lit. Another character that has been picked up on by a medium visiting St Anne's is that of a man from the 1300s dressed in hunting gear. His residual energy has been picked up in a bedroom in the building and he is said to have followed the black arts. The same medium also picked up on the energy of another spirit whilst in this room. The medium went into a trance and the voice of a spirit called 'Anne' came through her. It appeared that Anne was a young girl who had been tried

A pipe-smoking man is amongst the ghosts said to haunt the bar at St Anne's Castle Inn. (Photograph by Kelly Day)

as a witch. As tears ran down the medium's face, the voice claimed to have asked 'Mary' to help her. It continued: 'I pray my end is soon and the pain is not too much. I have had a good life in this place.' The evidence points to the fact that the medium may very well have also picked up on the spirit of Anne Huwghes, much like the paranormal investigators who had visited the inn previously.

With such a strong link to the 'dark arts' through the less than Christian phantom monks, the ghostly huntsman 'Satanist' and the spirit of a witch all allegedly residing within the pub, it is no surprise that so much paranormal activity continues at St Anne's Castle Inn. Perhaps the fact that the actual Scrapfaggot Stone (see The Scrapfaggot Poltergeist section of this book) is believed to now be located in the pub's car park may also be a contributing factor to the darker side of the inn's haunting.

The Scrapfaggot Green Poltergeist – Various Locations, Great Leighs, Chelmsford

In 1621, Ann Huwghes from Great Leighs was brought to trial at Chelmsford assizes for various misdemeanours pertaining to practicing witchcraft. Ann was found guilty and sentenced to death. Contrary to common belief, those found guilty of such crimes were not burned at the stake during this period of time, they were hung. However, the crimes Ann Huwghes was found guilty of included the murder of her husband, which was considered petty treason and was punishable by burning at the stake. It is said that Ann was burned at the stake and buried on the spot. A large stone was then placed over her grave to prevent her spirit from rising again. There is no official record of where Ann's execution and burial took place but traditionally those accused of witchcraft were buried at a crossroads. Many believe that the site of Ann Huwghes' grave was located at the crossroads of Scrapfaggot Green, in Great Leighs itself. The crossroads at Scrapfaggot Green had a large stone located at the site and villagers believed that the stone

marked the grave of a local witch (possibly Ann Huwghes), who had been burned at the stake there and whilst the stone remained over her grave the witch would remain trapped.

Incidentally, Scrapfaggot is an old Essex name for a witch and is possibly a corruption of the archaic Suffolk term for a witch: 'Scratch-Faggot'.

Three hundred and twenty-three years after Ann Huwghes' execution, the American Army were in the country to aid their English allies during the Second World War. This included a unit of American soldiers that were based in Great Leighs. Following their deployment to the village in October 1944 the soldiers discovered that Dratchett Lane, the road that went over the crossroads at Scrapfaggot Green, was too narrow for them to navigate their vehicles along. Unfamiliar with local superstition an officer gave the order for his men to widen the road and a G.I. was given the task of driving a bulldozer along the lane. In the process of carrying out his duties the soldier displaced the two ton witches stone, an action that is said to have led to a bizarre series of paranormal events throughout the village.

Amongst the first places to report strange happenings was the church of St Mary The Virgin in Great Leighs, situated along the road between St Anne's Castle Inn and The Dog and Gun pub. Shortly after the witch's stone had been disturbed the tenor bell in the church tower began tolling in the early hours of the morning of its own accord. The bell ropes then began playing reversed chimes on a Sunday. The church tower clock began acting erratically, striking midnight at two thirty in the morning and then losing an hour every day, something that had never happened before.

The villagers themselves then began witnessing bizarre events, many of them

The Church of St Mary the Virgin, in Great Leighs, during the Scrapfaggot Green Poltergeist incident of the 1940s. (Courtesy of www.harrypricewebsite.co.uk)

The Church of St Mary the Virgin, in 2011. (Photograph by Kelly Day)

involving their pets and livestock. Cows were giving birth prematurely and hens had stopped laying eggs; village sheep had strayed through unbroken hedges and chickens had escaped from locked fowl houses. There were even more disturbing happenings such as chickens, which nobody claimed to have lost, being found drowned in water-butts and a villager called Chipping discovered his rabbit sitting on eggs in a chicken coop. The landlord of St Anne's Castle Inn, Alfred Sykes, claimed that three geese had vanished from his garden although the enclosure they were kept in was undamaged. Farmers also found their haystacks being mysteriously toppled over during the night and corn stalks disappearing. only to be found later in adjacent meadows.

Other businesses were also being affected. A builder complained that a pile of scaffolding poles had been strewn about his yard like matchsticks and a local decorator found a dozen paint pots, brushes and other equipment under the beds in a cottage his men had been working in, even though they had stacked them neatly away the previous evening. The landlord of the Dog and Gun in Great Leighs, Mr Reynolds, had remained sceptical of the so called 'paranormal activity' going on in the village thus far. His mind was changed, somewhat, when he discovered a two hundred pound boulder deposited outside his front door. Upon inspection he found that the stone was of irregular shape, much worn and had no signs of moss or moisture on it; nobody

The landlord of St Anne's Castle Inn reported poltergeist activity during the Scrapfaggot Green incident. (Photograph by Kelly Day)

had lost or recognised the stone and its origin remained untraced.

More and more villagers came forward to report their stories, including a widow called Mrs Warren who went to bed one evening, only to find that all of her books had had their jackets changed by the following morning.

The story of the strange events in Great Leighs had now spread and the press began to take an interest. News reached a reporter from the *Sunday Pictorial* newspaper and he in turn contacted the famous psychical researcher Harry Price. Price received a phone call

Church bells rang out at odd hours and the church clock lost time at St Mary the Virgin Church, for no apparent reason. (Photograph by Kelly Day)

regarding the case on 6 October 1944, and visited Great Leighs on 11 October.

Upon arriving, Price was told that the previous evening chickens in a yard and rabbits in a hutch had mysteriously changed places despite the fasteners on their pens being undisturbed. Price was also informed that only a few hours before his arrival thirty sheep and two horses had been found dead in a field.

Price spent his time investigating various locations in Great Leighs, including St Mary's Church and St Annes Castle Inn where the landlord, Mr Sykes, had also reported poltergeist activity in an upstairs room. Price also examined the boulder that had been found outside the Dog and Gun pub by Mr Reynolds. Following his investigation the locals asked Price what they should do to cease the disturbances;

his reply was that if they thought the witch was responsible for the poltergeist activity then they should replace the stone over her grave at the crossroads.

According to Price's records the stone was replaced during a ceremony at midnight on 11-12 October 1944, with the stone being placed east and west. Price then reports that the paranormal activity ceased. A differing account appeared in *Times Magazine* on 23 October 1944. The magazine's account reports that the stone was replaced at midnight on 13 October 1944. The article describes how the villagers heaved the stone back into place, laying it north to south. The following morning the stone was moved once more and faggots from a nearby oak were laid out across the stone, spelling the word '*non in sum*'. Locals were perplexed at how the stone had

An alleged piece of the Witch's Stone, now found at St Anne's Castle Inn, Great Leighs. (Photograph by Kelly Day)

moved and as to what the message meant. An American G.I. based nearby translated the Latin for the villagers and explained that the message meant 'Nobody Home'. Whichever account is true the disturbances eventually petered out and it would seem that the Scrapfaggot Poltergeist had indeed been laid to rest for the time being.

Paranormal investigator Harry Price concluded that the Scrapfaggot Green phenomena was partly genuine, partly the work of a practical joker and partly due to mass-hysteria. Dr D.J.G. MacSweeney, an Irish expert in the paranormal who had also investigated the case (for the United Press), also released his findings. MacSweeney said:

> The witch legend is a matter for hooting and disbelief in adjoining Little Waltham. Little Walthamites in road crews assure me they have moved the stone a score of times in as many years. It is my reluctant conclusion that the witch of Scrapfaggot Green is – to be blunt – a hoax.

During the 1980s, a story broke out that the stone had been brought to St Anne's Castle Inn in Great Leighs in 1945 and laid near the car park. One night, three men from the pub tried to carry off the stone – still known as the witch's stone – but were unsuccessful. Upon investigation, the stone was found to be too small to be the same one that covered the witch's grave; but, it may well have been a fragment of the original stone. There is the possibility that the bulldozer that widened the road could quite easily have broken the stone and a piece found its way to the pub. It was also said that when the stone was originally moved from the crossroads bones and ashes were found beneath where the stone had laid.

If it is true that part of the witch's stone is the stone that lies near to St Anne's Castle Inn car park perhaps that may explain the paranormal activity that is said to occur to this day at the building. Could the poltergeist activity that occurs at the inn be attributed to the Scrapfaggot Green Poltergeist having found a new home?

The Grey Cat and Old Ruffy – The Beehive Pub, Barrack Lane, Great Waltham, Chelmsford

The Beehive pub in Great Waltham is said to have two rather different spirits; the first of which has been seen running down the corridor and disappearing into a bathroom wall. This sighting would have been strange enough; the fact that the spectre seen was not that of a human but that of a grey cat makes it even more mysterious.

The pub is also said to have another, rather more malicious spirit within its walls. This entity, unlike the phantom cat, has yet to be seen. The reason the spirit has not been seen is that it is said to be the pub's resident poltergeist. The poltergeist, known as 'Old Ruffy' is believed to have a particular fondness for breaking glasses in the bar and causing general disruption.

Prediction from the Grave – Langley Manor, Great Waltham, Chelmsford

Langley Manor is a large red brick building set in parkland overlooking Great Waltham. The site was first recorded in 1200 as a mill named Marshall, which was later changed by new owners to Langley. Around 1500, the house passed into the ownership of the Everard family. Members of the family included Sir Anthony and his wife Anne. Anne died in 1609 and Sir Anthony died in 1614, both were laid to rest beneath a tomb in Great Waltham Church. In 1710, the estate was sold to a family of London merchants named Tufnell and it was during this time that the house was rebuilt (completed in 1721) and the extensive gardens and parkland were laid out. Several public footpaths cross the park and afford fine views of the house and outbuildings, but the gardens and house are private and are not open to the public.

There is a legend attached to Langley Manor that sometime in the past a young girl was kidnapped from the estate and never found. More alarmingly the perpetrator is said to have been an apparition. The origins and details of this story have been lost over the years.

A far more detailed and documented haunting occurred at the Manor in the seventeenth century. The events that unfolded were relayed by Sir Charles Lee and documented by the Bishop of Gloucester.

During the 1600s, Sir Charles Lee had a daughter to his first wife who had sadly died during childbirth. His wife's sister, Lady Everard, had the girl educated until she was of a marriageable age. In the years that followed a partner was found for the girl, who had now become a young woman, and she was due to marry Sir William Perkins. Due to the events that unfolded one evening in 1662 at Langley Manor, the marriage never happened.

Sir Charles' daughter was living at Langley Manor with her aunt, Lady Everard, whilst her father was in Warwickshire. One Thursday evening the young woman had retired to her bed chamber and was drifting off to sleep. During her slumber she awoke to see what she thought was a bright, flick-ering light in the room. She knocked for the maid, who promptly came to her room. The woman asked the maid why there was a candle burning in her bedchamber whilst she was trying to sleep, to which the maid replied that there was no candle in the room except for the one the maid had brought with her when she was called. The woman then said that the light was perhaps the dying embers of the fire in the bedchamber; the maid replied that the fire in the fireplace was quite out and had been for a long time. The maid then surmised that she must have been dreaming, to which the woman agreed and excused the maid. After the maid departed the woman composed herself and fell back to sleep.

At 2 a.m. Sir Charles' daughter stirred from her sleep again and this time there was something far more frightening awaiting her. As she opened her eyes she saw the ghost of a little old woman stood beside her bed. The apparition was stood beside her pillow just in front of the curtains. As Sir Charles' daughter lay motionless in her bed, frozen by fear, the apparition began to speak to her. The ghost explained that she was, in fact, the woman's mother. She told her that she was very happy because by noon that day her daughter would be with her. The old woman then faded away before the woman's eyes. Eventually, the woman was able to compose herself enough to knock for the maid, who dutifully came to her bedchamber as summoned. The woman told the maid to fetch her clothes and help her dress. Once the woman was out of bed and dressed she went into her closet and stayed there until the morning.

Just after 9 a.m. the woman left the safety of her closet carrying a letter for her father. She took the letter to her aunt and explained to her what had occurred the evening before. She also instructed her aunt to send the letter to her father as soon as she passed away. Naturally, Lady Everard thought that her niece had been in some way mentally disturbed by her experience or was suffering from some kind of illness, so she sent to Chelmsford for both a surgeon and a physician. Both professionals arrived immediately and an examination of the young lady took place. The physician could find nothing medically wrong with her and was quite perplexed as to why she would be thinking that she was going to die.

Having being examined, and with the time approaching noon, the woman wanted a chaplain calling and one was sent for. The chaplain arrived at Langley Manor and read prayers with the woman. As soon as prayers were over the woman picked up her guitar and sat in a chair that had no arms. She began playing her instrument and singing along. As she did so, her aunt, the physician, the surgeons and others looked on. Just before 12 p.m. the woman put her guitar down, stood up and walked over to another chair in the room that had arms. She slumped down in the chair, took a laboured breath or two and died on the spot. The physician and surgeon rushed over to the woman but nothing could be done for her. The medical men were also astonished at how quickly her body had gone cold.

The letter the woman had written in the early hours of that morning was sent to her father, Sir Charles in Warwickshire. He was so affected by the loss of his daughter that he did not return to Langley Manor, or Great Waltham, until after she was buried. When he did return, Sir Charles ordered that his daughter's body be exhumed and laid to rest with her mother, as she had requested in the letter she had written to him the day that she died.

The Rose and Crown Poltergeist – The Rose and Crown, Minnow's End, Great Waltham, Chelmsford

During the 1980s, The Rose and Crown in Great Waltham was subject to a mild poltergeist infestation. During a period of conversion work, builders reported being plagued by bizarre disturbances. This included tools being left in one location and turning up in another and unexplained noises on the site.

Following the completion of the work there were no further reports of poltergeist activity.

The Ghost of Lady Alice – Graces Manor, Little Baddow, Chelmsford

Great Graces (or 'Graces Manor' as it is also known) was built in the sixteenth century and is set in thirteen acres of land in view of the Chelmer Valley. Located in Little Baddow, the manor had passed through several hands by 1577, before finally being sold to Arthur Herrys for £1,800 in 1591. By 1612, Sir Henry Mildmay had bought Great Graces and settled there. Sir Henry was a war veteran and had fought in the wars in Ireland, where he was knighted at Dublin Castle in 1612. He had also had an illustrious political career, having been Member of Parliament for Maldon three times, Sheriff of Essex in 1628 and Deputy Lieutenant of the County.

Sir Henry was married twice, his first wife being Alice Harris (Alice being something of a 'child bride' at the time of their marriage). One morning in 1615 the usually charming Lady Alice forlornly descended the staircase at Graces Manor and left the building.

She walked along a lane, flanked by trees until she came to an area just upstream of Cuton Lock named Sandon Brook. It was here that after six years of marriage the young Lady drowned herself. Her explanation being that her husband had been 'unkind to her'.

Sir Henry married again and he himself died in 1637. He was buried beside his first wife Alice. Sir Henry left the sum of £40 in his will to his second wife's brother, John Gurdon, to have a monument erected in the Parish Church of St Mary the Virgin in Little Baddow. The elaborate monument was erected on the north side of the chancel of the church and is known as the Mildmay monument. The stone effigy portrays Sir Henry in a recumbent position, clad in his armour. At his feet are his two wives.

Ever since the death of Lady Alice, the lane that she walked along that fateful day has been known as Grace's Walk, and ever since then Lady Alice is also believed to haunt the area too.

In a post on the website www.francis-frith.com, Gemma Hooper recounted:

I was born in Little Baddow and was familiar with the story of Alice Mildmay and Jesse Berridge's book. One summer night, three of us rode ponies down Riffhams Close to Great Graces and down Grace's Walk, arriving at midnight. We crossed the bridge and all I can remember is that after that all three ponies turned and galloped back up towards the house.

One of the more recent paranormal encounters at Grace's Walk occurred one evening in November 2001. A young couple moored their houseboat near Grace's Walk and settled down for the night.

Whilst relaxing on the boat they heard the sound of footsteps on the roof and what sounded like gravel being thrown at the walls. As they looked out they also saw mysterious lights flashing around the boat. Disturbed by their experience the male witness went out to investigate, expecting to find mischievous teenagers or worse. As he investigated around the towpath the witness found nothing; there was nobody in sight. Even more alarming was the fact that there was no gravel or stones along the path either. He returned to the boat and the perplexed and terrified couple decided to leave and steered their vessel away from the area immediately. The following morning they returned the boat to the owner of the local boat company and related their experience to him. It was only then that they heard the story of Alice Mildmay and realised they may have had their own encounter with the ghost of Grace's Walk.

The Little Leighs Bodysnatchers – St John the Evangelist Churchyard, Church Lane, Little Leighs, Chelmsford

Many graveyards are believed to be haunted, just by the very nature of what they are. The graveyard at St John the Evangelist Church in Little Leighs is one of several in the county of Essex where it is said that spirits reside. Over the years, many unusual sights and sounds have been witnessed there and some would say with very good reason, for this particular graveyard was the scene of an event that was so shocking it literally raised the dead.

Before the Anatomy Act of 1832, the only legal supply of corpses for anatomical

The ghost of Lady Alice. (Illustration by Tracie Wayling)

research purposes in Britain were those of criminals that were found guilty at trial and then condemned to death and dissection by the law. This caused a huge problem for medical schools during a time of rapid expansion. The conviction and sentencing rate during this period was around fifty-five people a year, with medical establishments requiring as many as 500 cadavers a year to carry out their research and teaching. This was also a period when the refrigeration of bodies was virtually non-existent, therefore making long term storage of bodies virtually impossible as they would decay rapidly and become unusable for study. There was, however, a rather dubious and horrific solution to the problem and it came in the form of a new kind of criminal. These men were more than prepared to help supply the demand of medical science in a grisly trade that became known as bodysnatching.

During this 'boom time' in the trading of corpses, security had been stepped up in the graveyards of the major towns and cities. Not to be deterred from their lucrative activities the bodysnatchers were prepared to move further a field to obtain their commodities. The crimes were now being committed in the unguarded churchyards of small towns and villages, including those in Chelmsford.

In 1823, Little Leighs had a population of 160 residents. Of those people, nine were buried in the same year, three of which occurred in December 1823. The deceased were Susannah Knight, aged thirty (buried 14 December), Abraham Leader, aged thirty-three (buried 21 December) and Johanna Chinnery, aged twenty-four (buried 22 December). The village itself lies along the old Roman Road (now the A131) between Braintree and Chelmsford. In 1823, the road was a turnpike and consequently had a toll-gate across it. Following the tollgate was a junction that led off to a field with a gate that was known as Lower Reedings, in one direction, and the road, which is now known as Church Lane, in the other. Half a mile along Church Lane is St John's Church and also the graveyard that the deceased were buried in.

At 5 a.m. on Friday 26 December 1823, Charles Rogers was making his way home to Felstead. Being superstitious Rogers did not want to walk through the graveyard at St John's so he made a detour towards Lower Reedings. As he made his way across the field he discovered a horse and cart; the horse was tied to a tree by a whip. Rogers looked around and could see nobody in the vicinity so he made his way to the turnpike and told the toll collector, John Redwood what he had found. Rogers and Redwood returned to the field and inspected the cart. Inside were an umbrella, food for both the driver and a horse and a pair of dirty pantaloons.

The men took the horse and cart to the nearby St Anne's Castle Inn where they told the landlord, John Crisp, what had happened. They left the horse and cart in the safekeeping of Crisp and instructed him that if anyone came to claim them as their property perhaps he had better try and make sure they gave him good evidence that this was the case before handing the horse and cart over; the time was now around 6 a.m. Two hours later, Crisp was talking to a man named Francis when they were interrupted by a man inquiring about the horse and cart. The man was called Samuel Clark and he told Crisp that he had been drinking ale and eating toast the previous evening and become rather drunk. It was then that he decided it may be best if he did not continue his journey home that evening.

So he found a field, tied up his horse and lay down to sleep off the drink. When he awoke his horse and cart had gone. He had then approached the inn and saw the horse and cart there. After confirming the contents of the cart with him Crisp was satisfied with Clark's story. Clark paid Crisp for the hay, Crisp handed the horse and cart back over to him and Clark headed off towards Braintree.

The story of the morning's discoveries had created a bit of a stir locally and interest had become aroused. Blacksmith John Broomfield lived near the tollgate and had heard about recent events, so he decided to visit Lower Reedings field to see what he could find for himself. Amongst the branches of the tree that the horse had been tied to, Broomfield found a shovel. Spurred by the discovery he then looked around

The Little Leighs bodysnatcher, Samuel Clark. (Illustration by Jason Day)

the adjacent field, Church Brooms. Whilst inspecting Church Brooms, Broomfield came upon a sack that was doubled over. Printed on the sack were the words J. Harvey, Crayford Mill. As Broomfield picked up the sack two loaded pistols fell out and onto the floor. Broomfield then went to find the owner of the field, church warden Hugh Simons. Simons returned with Broomfield to the spot where the sack was found. Barely twelve feet away, they made a much more startling discovery; a woman's body lay in the ground partly covered by earth.

Fearing that a murderer was on the loose the men set off to raise the alarm. Their journey took them through St John's churchyard and it was there that they discovered the earth of Johanna Chinnery's grave had been desecrated and her burial clothes strewn around. She had been buried there four days previously.

The whereabouts of Clark was immediately sought and he was found in nearby Broomfield, drinking in the Kings Arms public house. Upon his capture he denied any knowledge of the pistols and stuck to his story. Later investigations found that he had been seen before; acting suspiciously in the area with another man and common belief was that Clark had remained in the area with intent to recover the body at a later time.

Suspicious that other graves may have been disturbed, magistrates ordered that further graves of the recently buried be inspected. On Wednesday 31 December 1823 the graves of Abraham Leader and Susannah Knight were exhumed. Both coffins were opened and found to be empty except for the funeral shrouds that had been torn from their bodies.

Samuel Clark was charged with taking the bodies of Abraham Leader, Susannah Knight and Johanna Chinnery. He was also accused of stealing the clothes that Johanna Chinnery was buried in. Clark appeared before the court on Friday 23 January 1824, the three indictments of bodysnatching had no evidence presented to the court so, therefore, he was found not guilty on all three accounts. Of the charge of stealing Johanna Chinnery's burial clothes however, Clark was found guilty. He was sentenced to be transported for seven years.

Johanna Chinnery was laid to rest once more, yet the bodies of Abraham Leader and Susannah Knight were never found.

This episode of history presents facts to us that may indeed hold the key to the identity of the spirits that reside within the churchyard of St John the Evangelist in Little Leighs. Perhaps the spirits of Abraham Leader or Susannah Knight are wandering the grounds looking to find peace in the place they were originally laid to rest. Could Johanna Chinnery be patrolling the area, trying to make sure another unfortunate soul is not disturbed from their eternal sleep as she was? Maybe, just maybe, Samuel Clark, or indeed whoever stole the bodies from the graveyard, has returned from the afterlife to try and continue his ghastly crimes.

Stranger in a Parka – Little Waltham, Chelmsford

One evening, in the early 2000s, a young lady named Kate was driving through the Little Waltham area of Chelmsford. She parked her car and sat chatting with her friend. Everything appeared to be normal when suddenly Kate's friend looked out of through the car windscreen, jumped up out of the passenger seat and exclaimed, 'What the hell is that?'

Reacting immediately to the look of horror on her friend's face, Kate turned on the car headlights. Illuminating the darkness the lights revealed that there was nothing in front of the vehicle. Reeling from her experience, Kate's friend urged her to drive away from the area. Still none the wiser as to what her friend had seen Kate started the car and they drove away. As they drove towards a local fast food outlet Kate's friend described to her what had happened. As they had been talking her friend had noticed something moving in the darkness outside in front of the car. She turned to get a better look and was confronted by the sight of a bald headed man in a long, green parka or anorak style jacket. The friends stopped off at the fast food restaurant and then Kate dropped her friend off at her home, around six miles from where she had seen the mysterious figure.

Kate headed off home herself, driving along the back roads from her friend's house. As she passed through the Little Waltham area she saw a figure ahead of her in the distance. Kate dipped her headlights as she approached the figure and turned to get a better look. Walking along the road was a bald headed man in a long, green anorak jacket. As Kate passed him the man stared intensely back at her. She looked back towards the figure through her rear-view mirror and the man had vanished. Kate was convinced there was no way a person could have disappeared from view in such a short space of time.

Kate consulted her friend and they agreed that they had both seen the same eerie figure that evening on two separate occasions in Little Waltham. Who, or indeed what, he was remains unknown.

The stranger in a parka, witnessed by two women in one evening. (Illustration by Tracie Wayling)

An unusual entity is said to haunt Springfield Place. (Photograph by Kelly Day)

The Malevolent Gnome – Springfield Place, Springfield, Chelmsford

Between 1864 and 1946 reports came in from Springfield Place of a very unusual haunting indeed. There were several witnesses that, on separate occasions, attested to being harassed by an unknown force whilst at the building. Objects were also being thrown from shelves during this time, similar to the activity often associated with a poltergeist infestation, with much of the activity occurring within the panelled Blue Room.

In 1946, Springfield Place was requisitioned for use as a girl's hostel and according to witness testimony the haunting continued. Two girls sleeping on the top floor of the building reported being awoken by something touching their faces. They were so frightened by the experience that they immediately jumped out of their beds to report the incident.

Based on evidence and eyewitness reports researchers believe the assailant to be 'an ugly, little, dwarf-like gnome' who is believed to haunt Springfield Place and the surrounding area, particularly the churchyard.

Two

The Ghosts of Chelmsford:

The Surrounding Area

The Vague Form – The Angel Inn – Notley Road, Braintree

The reported haunting at the Angel Inn dates back to the 1960s; with the following twenty years being the most paranormally active to date. During this twenty year period mysterious footsteps were heard within the building and dogs were known to bark and become unnerved with no apparent cause for the change in their temperament.

The Angel Inn, Braintree. (Photograph by Jason Day)

The most intriguing account to be relayed during this time was an eyewitness report of an apparition being seen on the stairway. The spirit manifested itself as a vague form before disappearing into thin air.

The Garage Ghosts – Autoparts, Rayne Road, Braintree

It is not only ancient castles, medieval churches and old inns that are purported to be haunted. There are many more modern locations that have reported paranormal activity within their walls, as is the case of Autoparts shop in Braintree.

Autoparts first came to the attention of paranormal investigators when a group were investigating the Horse and Groom pub across the road. A witness who worked at the Horse and Groom had observed an apparition of a lady walk from the pub, across the road and into the Autoparts building. Following the conclusion of their investigation of the Horse and Groom the investigators decided to follow up on the information they had received and visit Autoparts themselves.

Andy Radley, a member of the Essex Ghost Hunting Team, visited Autoparts and enquired as to whether any of the staff had witnessed the phantom lady or indeed any other paranormal activity within the building. Employees at the shop were more than willing to recount their numerous experiences to Andy. On several occasions a phantom lady had been seen entering

A young girl is believed to haunt Autoparts in Braintree. (Photograph by Kelly Day)

the building through the front of the shop and exiting through a wall that had formerly been a side door. Other paranormal phenomena had also been experienced; this included several compact discs that had gone missing from the shop floor, never to be found again. Andy inquired as to whether the owners of the building would be receptive to his team investigating the premises and they responded that they would.

On January 27 2011, Andy returned to Autoparts with the other members of the Essex Ghost Hunting Team to carry out a paranormal investigation of the building. Throughout the evening the team carried out various experiments in attempts to both communicate with any spirits that may have been in the building and to capture any evidence of a haunting. During the vigils, the team's mediums claimed to have 'tapped into' the residual energy of four or five spirits, including a woman called Mary Parish. The team also claimed to have communicated with at least one spirit that was actually present within the building at the time. Using a pendulum to communicate with the spirits, the team made contact with what they believed was the ghost of a young girl. Based on the yes or no answers given by the movement of the pendulum it was established that the girl's name was Margaret. Margaret was seven years old and had an older brother called Edward. According to the team's communication with Margaret's spirit, Margaret often stands by an upstairs window in the building looking for her mother. During this experiment a team member experienced the feeling of a presence behind her and the sensation of someone, or something, blowing on her neck.

The team investigated the whole building with mixed results. A compact disc which was set up as a trigger object was found to have not moved during the inves-

tigation and other experiments conducted on the ground floor of the building also reaped no conclusive evidence of paranormal activity. Interestingly, the coldest room in the building that night was the workshop, even though this was the only room in the building that was insulated.

The first floor proved to be the most active, especially the front bedroom above the shop. As the investigation drew to a conclusion one of the team heard a noise coming from one of the other rooms. They described the sound as being 'like a spring hitting something'. The room was believed to have been empty at the time so the team went to investigate. Upon entering the room they discovered that it was indeed empty, but strangely enough there was a spring sat in the middle of the floor. The spring had not been there when the team initially looked around the building at the beginning of the investigation and staff at the shop confirmed that there were no springs kept in that room either.

Upon researching their findings the team discovered that a Mary Parish did live in Braintree between 1861 and 1871. Unfortunately no records could be found to confirm that she had lived in the building that is now the Autoparts shop. Similarly, the full identity of little Margaret has yet to be confirmed too.

The Haunted Pub – The Horse and Groom, Rayne Road, Braintree

In the winter of 2010, one of the owners of the Horse and Groom pub in Braintree approached a local medium regarding the strange occurrences they believed were going on in the building. Amongst the paranormal phenomena experienced at the pub were unexplained noises, strange smells

Essex Ghost Hunting Team investigated the Horse and Groom in 2010. (Photograph by Kelly Day)

and even the sighting of an apparition. On one occasion a member of staff claimed to have seen a phantom lady walk across the road from the pub to another premises. The apparition was then seen sat in an upstairs room, staring out of a window. Staff and customers alike had borne witness to these and other anomalies, and it was with this in mind that the owners had sought help in getting to the bottom of it.

On the 17 December 2010, the Essex Ghost Hunting Team arrived at the location. The team comprised of both paranormal investigators and mediums (including the medium that had been approached by the owner). The team were met by members of staff from the pub that were to accompany them throughout the investigation. Upon entering the building, one of the team's mediums, Andy, believed that he had picked up the spirit of a little girl that was making a snorting noise in the bar area. Both the team and staff quickly began to experience a feeling of extreme discomfort in the room and decided to continue their investigation in another part of the building. The group then made their way upstairs along the maze like corridors, during which time several people reported hearing unexplained noises which nobody could account for.

Having arrived at the front bedroom, one of the team's mediums believed they had picked up the spirit of an old lady sat in an armchair. Photographs taken in the room at the time revealed that some orbs had been captured within the images. (Some paranormal investigators believe that orbs are the result of the first stages of a spirit trying to manifest itself using energy from within the location.) Some of the people present in the room began feeling a 'squeezing' pressure on their heads. Given the oppressive nature of the energy in the room they decided to head back downstairs and into the cellar. Whilst in the cellar the team believed they encountered a third spirit, a man who was stood in the corner smoking a pipe. Staff confirmed that the ghostly figure of a man had previously been seen in the cellar on more than one occasion.

The group returned to the bar area, where medium and founder of Essex Ghost Hunters, Andy Radley, once again encountered the ghostly girl. This time Andy alleged to have made contact with the girl, he said the girl liked to play hide and seek in the pool room and kitchen areas of the pub. Interestingly, Andy also said the girl's name was Eliza Pigging or Piggot and that is why he had picked up on her making a snorting noise when he entered the pub. It was decided the team would head into the pool room.

Whilst in the pool room several members of the group said they could smell freshly baked bread. One of the staff members present recalled that one of the regulars in the pub had reported smelling the same thing in that area of the building in the past. The group decided to form a circle in order to try and communicate with any spirits that were present and began a séance. The group held hands and almost immediately began swaying. With little success during this experiment, the team were just about to leave the pool room and return to the bar when one of their EMF meters recorded a significant reading. One of the accompanying members of staff from the pub then felt a tickling sensation in her lower back, despite the fact that no other person present had touched her. Despite these interesting occurrences there was no further activity in the pool room so the group returned to the bar area. The team mediums began trying to communicate with

the spirits within the building once more and once again Eliza allegedly came through. Amongst the information she imparted was the fact that her father was a baker. The team concluded their investigation and endeavoured to analyse their findings.

Upon conducting some research, Essex Ghost Hunting Team investigator and researcher Wendy Sharman found some very interesting results. She found that there had indeed been an Eliza Piggin in Braintree. Eliza was the daughter of Samuel and Rebbeca Piggin and was born in 1823. Samuel was a baker and innkeeper of the Bird in the Hand in Braintree. Their son (also Samuel) had also had a daughter named Eliza who was born in 1844. Samuel had had two wives (Hannah and Harriet) and was the innkeeper of the Bird in the Hand and later the Horse and Groom in 1851, where he lived with his family.

In 2011, psychic photographer Ron Bowers visited the Horse and Groom at the invitation of the owners to see if he could pick up on any spirit energy that may have been present. Ron claimed to have sensed something on a previous visit to the pub and was only too happy to return to investigate. Ron claims to use 'mediumship with his camera' and capture images of spirits through it. During his visit to the Horse and Groom, Ron believes he captured the images of a spirit stood in the kitchen area.

The image contains a blurry figure stood near some tables. To all intents and purposes the image does indeed look like what you would expect a 'ghost' to be. Upon the release of the picture, through the local newspaper, etc. controversy ensued. There has been much debate as to the authenticity of the photograph due to its content, and due to the questionability of the legitimacy of spirit photography itself. As is the case with a lot of evidence that is presented as proof of the paranormal, there are those that support the evidence and those that are sceptical of it. Future analysis of the image and investigation of the building itself may one day reveal the secrets of the Horse and Groom.

The Strange Mist – 47 Church Street, Coggeshall

The former inn at 47 Church Street encountered paranormal activity from 1966 onwards, when residents at the building reported odd smells, doors opening and closing of their own accord, and a strange mist that crossed the base of the stairs.

The Unknown Presence – The Old Black Boy Bistro, Church Street, Coggeshall

In 2010, the proprietors of the Old Black Boy Bistro in Coggeshall reported unexplained occurrences within their establishment. The couple had witnessed strange lights and phantom sounds inside the building but things escalated when they claimed to have seen a spectral figure in their bedroom. Things became unbearable when physical phenomena began occurring and one of the proprietors believed they had been touched by an unseen entity. The frightened family sought help and contacted the Essex Ghost Hunting Team.

Following an initial consultation, the team of paranormal investigators and mediums returned to the Bistro in October 2010 to carry out an investigation. After several vigils and experiments the team picked up a lot of information and evidence. More importantly, following the teams visit, the proprietors of the establishment feel a lot more comfortable in their property.

Phantom Monks – Coggeshall Abbey Ruins, Coggeshall

Coggeshall Abbey was founded as a Savigniac house in around 1140 by Queen Matilda, wife of King Stephen. She had inherited the manor of Coggeshall and endowed it to the new abbey. It proved an ideal ready-made site for the Cistercian order when it took over in 1147, having absorbed the impoverished Savigniac order and all of its houses. Coggeshall Abbey was demolished in 1538 as the Dissolution of Monasteries swept across the country, although some of the abbey's structures did survive, mostly as ruins. By 1581, Anne Paycocke and her husband Richard Benyan acquired the abbey ruins and built the east wing of the present Abbey House around the remains of the abbey's infirmary. Of the abbey church and the buildings, all that survives now are foundations and buried remains, except for parts of the eastern wing, the guesthouse and the abbot's lodgings that still stand. According to eyewitness reports, a ghostly wrinkled monk silently walks these sites and ruins with a lit taper in his hands, making his way along old lanes and heading towards the Blackwater River. Phantom monks have also been sighted at Cradle House, a former haven for clergymen who held meetings in secret rooms within the building. These spirits have been seen dancing in the garden of the building.

The Lights and the Old Man – Guild House – Market End, Coggeshall

Another building that has experienced paranormal activity in the village of Coggeshall is Guild House at Market End. A small old man has reputedly materialised at the foot of a bed in the master bedroom, and strange balls of lights have been observed drifting around in the attic, through the window, by independent witnesses from outside the building.

The Haunted Hotel – White Hart Hotel – Market End, Coggeshall

The White Hart, Coggeshall, was constructed in 1420 and still has a wealth of its original features, notably its attractive timbered rooms. The main part was built in 1526 as a home for one Robert Paycocke, but appears to have become an inn quite soon afterwards, patronised by merchants who dealt far and wide in the town's principal manufacture – lace. The oldest part of the building was originally one end of the Coggeshall's Guildhall which was later incorporated into the White Hart Hotel and is now its resident's lounge. It is this area of the pub that is said to be particularly haunted.

Little is known about the trapped soul that haunts this building, nobody knows the history behind who this may be or even which gender they are. Typical phenomena encountered in the building include sudden drops in temperature, a feeling of being watched and unexplained sounds.

A recent visit to the White Hart revealed a little more about the haunting. A member of staff recounted to me that televisions have been known to switch themselves off and objects are reguarly moved around by unknown forces. This phenomena is particuarly common in room 5.

Market End, the most haunted area of Coggeshall. (Photograph by Kelly Day)

The haunted White Hart Hotel in Coggeshall. (Photograph by Kelly Day)

Robin the Woodcutter – Robin's Brook, Coggeshall

One of Coggeshall's most famous ghosts is that of Robin the Woodcutter. Robin was said to have carved an image entitled 'Angel of the Christmas Mysteries' in the sixteenth century. The carving was hidden during the Reformation and never found. Robin's ghostly axe is still said to be heard chopping away in the distance, in the area of a brook in the village that is now known as Robins Brook. The phantom woodcutter has also been seen walking around the grounds of the Abbey, which is said to be haunted.

The Brasserie Prankster – Baumanns Brasserie, Stoneham Street, Coggeshall

Baumanns Brasserie is located in the village of Coggeshall, one of the most haunted villages in Essex. Not to be outdone by its neighbouring haunts, the sixteenth-century building has a spectacular haunted history all of its own.

During the 1980s, Mark Baumann was a 21-year-old chef working at Hintlesham Hall. During this time, Irish entrepreneur Peter Langan visited the establishment and sampled Baumann's cooking. Langan had previously gone into partnership with actor Michael Caine and opened Langan's

Brasserie in Piccadilly, London, to much acclaim. Langdon was so impressed by Baumann's skills that he quickly recruited him to help establish one of what would become a chain of Langan's Brasseries.

In 1986, Langan and Baumann opened the Langan's Brasserie in Coggeshall, Essex, with Baumann being the head chef. After a very successful two years tragedy struck the business when Langan died in December 1988, shortly after a fire at his home. Baumann took over the restaurant which then became Baumanns Brasserie.

Over the years there have been many reports of unexplained phenomena that have taken place within the building as Mr Baumann told reporters from the *Essex Chronicle* in September 2010:

> Strange Stuff has been going on for years, but it has really escalated in the past six months and certainly livened things up a bit. I don't believe in any kind of spiritual nonsense, but the things that have happened do leave a lot of unanswered questions.

Both staff and diners have reported a plethora of paranormal activity which left them both perplexed and unnerved. Unaccountable footsteps have been heard walking up and down the stairs at the Brasserie, even when the restaurant has been empty and staff accounted for. The main door to the restaurant has opened by itself as staff sat chatting; as they looked around expecting somebody to enter, they realised that nobody was there. There have also been several incidents of objects being moved by unseen hands, such as knives and forks moving across tables and salt and pepper shakers flying across the room. Door handles, fire extinguishers and even large furniture has been reported to have moved overnight with no apparent cause.

Much of the phenomena appear to occur around tables eight and twelve of the restaurant. Customers who have dined at these tables have reported feeling temperature drops or 'cold spots' and also hearing the sound of cutlery falling to the floor although, on inspection, the cutlery is still on the tables. Mark Baumann related that these two tables were regularly used by his departed friend and partner Peter Langan. Apparently, Langan would eat his dinner at table twelve before falling asleep, often inebriated, at table eight. This may well suggest that it is indeed the spirit of practical joker Langan (whose picture still overlooks table twelve) that could be haunting the building. In September 2010, Baumann went on to tell *Daily Gazette* reporters, 'He was always up to mischief and causing little bits of havoc and having fun.'

One particular incident of note involved a female guest at the restaurant. The woman in question was enjoying a meal when something very unusual occurred. She was wearing a gold watch that she had worn for more than twenty years and had never taken off. As she sat eating her meal she noticed the watch was unclasping. As she looked on in bewilderment the watch unclasped, fell to the floor and broke.

Another possible paranormal event that took place at Baumanns involved Mark Baumann himself. Baumann had invested in a picture of a white dog for the restaurant wall and upon delivery hung it in its new home. Shortly afterwards, the former owner of the painting visited Baumanns purely by chance. Whilst chatting about the picture the man explained that he had sold the painting as he had found the image of the dog to be quite eerie and unnerving. Just as he mentioned this, and without warning or obvious cause, the painting leapt from the wall and flew across the room.

All Saints' Church, Cressing. (Photograph by Kelly Day)

the evening, with beam barriers detecting movement and EMF meters showing significant readings. At one point during proceedings an EMF meter appeared to respond to questions being asked of the spirits by showing very apparent 'spikes' in the readings.

Along with evidence collected from the electrical equipment there was also a lot of information gathered by the team's mediums. The mediums believed that they identified up to five separate spirits in the building, one of which they identified as Peter Langan.

On a final note, when photographer Chris Rushton from the *Essex Chronicle* called in to Baumanns Brasserie to take a photograph for a related piece in the local newspaper, his camera flew from its tripod and landed on a table in the restaurant with no obvious cause.

Mark Baumann continued to keep a record of the alleged paranormal activity that was being reported at the restaurant and in September 2010 he agreed to allow a team of paranormal investigators to investigate the building. At 9 p.m. on 27 September 2010, investigators from the Essex Ghost Hunting Team arrived at Baumanns Brasserie and were joined by journalists from local newspapers. The team, journalists, Mark Baumann and his staff encountered several unusual occurrences during the investigation.

Upon entering the building, the Essex Ghost Hunting Team were greeted by the lights suddenly and inexplicably tripping out. Door handles were seen to move of their own volition and a refrigerator thermometer fluctuated between 1.9 and 4.2 degrees upon command. Mr Baumann and his staff attested to the fact that this kind of fluctuation with the thermometer had never happened before.

The investigators paranormal equipment also picked up interesting readings during

Phantom Music – The Parish Church of All Saints, Church Road, Cressing

There is a possibility that the Nave of The Parish Church of All Saints in Cressing dates back to the twelfth century, there is, however, firm proof that the Chancel dates back to the thirteenth century. The Grade I listed building certainly has a long and distinguished history, and during the mid 1900s the church encountered a brief spell of paranormal activity.

During the winter of 1949, several locals reported hearing the sound of the church organ playing. This of course would not be uncommon, except for the fact that it occurred whilst the church was locked and in darkness. This phenomenon has not been reported since, nor has any rational explanation ever been given as to why it occurred at the time.

Three

The Ghosts of Cressing Temple Barns, Witham & Beyond

Cressing Temple Barns takes its unusual name from the medieval monks of the Knights Templar, who founded the two vast wooden barns which form the centrepiece of this rural estate just outside of Braintree. The Barley Barn was built in around1190, the Wheat Barn in around 1250 —both are timber framed. To one side of the barns is the Walled Garden which is the result of painstaking research and archaeological excavation, and is filled with species widely cultivated in Tudor times. Other buildings

Cressing Temple Barns, as viewed from the gardens. (Photograph by Jason Day)

located within the grounds are a Tudor granary, a well house, a cart lodge and a seventeenth-century farm house.

The site was given to the Knights Templar by Matilda, wife of King Stephen, in 1137. The Knights Templar, a group of warrior monks, was created in 1119 to protect crusade pilgrims. After the Templars were suppressed, Cressing went to the Hospitallers (in 1312). In 1515, the farm was leased to a private owner and the estate passed through a number of owners in the succeeding years, including a former Lord Mayor of London. The estate eventually became a tenanted farm. In 1987, Cressing Temple was split up, with the farm buildings and surrounding land purchased by Essex County Council.

Throughout the past century several ghosts have been unearthed, some literally, at the barns. There are believed to be at least five different spirits haunting the

Several spirits have been encountered at this location. (Photograph by Kelly Day)

site, some have been witnessed recently and others are accounts that have been related through various sources over the years. Given the vast history and size of the estate it comes as no surprise that the ghosts of Cressing Temple Barns are as varied as they are intriguing.

One of the oldest ghosts that is said to haunt Cressing Temple is that of a Roman soldier. A story related to an employee at the site in 1986 recounted the tale of this particular apparition. The phantom Centurion is said to appear in the fields next to the barns, warning of the advance of Boudicca and her revolting troops. The soldier is said to have a head wound and appears to be in distress, apparently pleading for shelter and a direction to make good his escape from the pending onslaught.

During archaeological excavations in the gardens at the barns the remains of a Romano-British man were found.

Constructing the Wheat Barn at Cressing Temple. (Photograph by Kelly Day)

His head had been severed and placed on his feet in an east-west grave. Examination of the remains suggested that the man was an older adult, possibly more than 35-years-old when he died. Examination of the skull and other bones concluded that he had not died of decapitation and there was no evidence of cut marks. The head must have either fallen off or been surgically removed before burial. The man whose remains were discovered during the excavation became known as 'Lefty', as only the left side of his body remained buried to excavate. Could 'Lefty' and the bloodied soldier be the same man?

A former occupant of the farm house recalled hearing stories of a second spirit that was said to roam the grounds of the property. During his childhood, the man remembered hearing stories of the ghost of a knight being seen by witnesses during the early to mid-1900s. Legend had it that the night was buried somewhere within the Cressing Temple Barns estate.

Attempts were made to locate the knight's remains during the 1930s, when a dowser was brought in to search for him. Using divining rods, the dowser located an area near an old pump house that could have possibly been the final resting place of the knight. The location was excavated but no traces of evidence were uncovered. A 'proper' excavation was also carried out at the grounds in the 1930s but records of the findings may have possibly been lost. Interestingly, the Knights Templar were said to have hidden their treasures somewhere on the estate before being disbanded. Maybe the spectral knight is returning to the site to unearth the valuables he hid all those years ago.

A Templar Knight, a phantom knight is said to haunt the grounds of the Barns. (Photograph by Kelly Day)

The most celebrated of the Cressing Temple ghosts is that of the phantom cavalier whose presence was witnessed several times in the sixteenth-century farmhouse building during the 1970s and the early 1980s. The first reports of a haunting at the farmhouse were unveiled during the occupancy of farm manager Jim Stadden. Jim's son, then eight-years-old, described seeing a man at the top of the stairs during the 1970s. The child recounted that the man wore blue trousers and big boots. He also related that the figure wore a big dark hat and had long curly hair beneath it. The Stadden family eventually moved out of the farm house and left Cressing Temple Barns, the spirit that resided within the building however, decided to stay.

The Lidstone family were the last family to occupy the farm house at Cressing Temple Barns before Essex County Council acquired the property in 1987. Richard Lidstone was the farm manager and he and his family moved into the house during the early 1980s. Richard's wife recalled that during their occupancy of the farm house she had always regarded the building as somewhat creepy. The whole family felt uneasy when they used the backstairs of the house and tried to avoid the area when possible. Mrs Lidstone would always tentatively check around the corner of the doorway at the top of the stairs before walking around it, her son Liam was also particularly weary of the top of the stairs too. Mrs Lidstone also recollected that the main bathroom would go cold on occasion for no apparent reason – a common occurrence in haunted locations. The family were so unnerved by the general feel of the house that even Richard, the man

The Haunted Farmhouse at Cressing Temple Barns. (Photograph by Jason Day)

of the house, was affected by it. One incident that highlighted this occurred whilst the rest of the family were away for a short while. During their trip, Richard brought his dogs into the house until they returned. The dogs were never allowed into the house but Richard decided that he would rather allow them in whilst the family were away than be by himself in the building.

The Lidstone family had, so far, experienced strange occurrences within the house that could be attributed to paranormal phenomena, but by 1984 they were presented with evidence that pointed far more strongly towards proof of a haunting. The family's three-year-old son Liam was becoming more reluctant to approach the backstairs or the main stairway of the house and his mother was becoming concerned about her son's fears. When questioned about why he was scared of the stairs the talkative child gave her an answer she wasn't quite expecting.

Liam explained that he had seen a strange man on the stairs; he called him the Hall Man. The man had appeared at the top of the main staircase on the landing near the bathroom. He described the figure as having long dark hair and wearing a big floppy hat. He said the man wore dark trousers with a thin red stripe down them, similar to tracksuit bottoms, and carried a horn. Liam seemed to be more sensitive to the paranormal activity in the house and on another occasion his mother found him laying a table with several spaces. When she questioned him as to what he was doing Liam answered that it was for the men outside and that they ate lettuce.

Liam was so young at the time that he could not read or write and the family did not have a television in the house. In a bid to discover the Hall Man's identity, or to try and find out whether this was just their

child's imagination, the Lidstone's questioned Liam some more. He was shown a portrait of a Cavalier and Liam identified the Hall Man as looking like the man in the picture. The Hall Man was later seen several times in the bedrooms and the library of the house. The Lidstone family returned to Cressing Temple Barns on a visit in 1994, where they recounted some of their experiences to Barry J. Crouch, who archived the reports.

Research into the farm house's history revealed that Sir Thomas Davies. Kt. Lord Mayor of London took the estate in 1677, during the time of the English Civil War (1642 − 1680). His eldest son, Thomas Davies Esq. shot himself a year later. The family sold the estate in 1703. There are no firm records of where Thomas took his life on the estate, or indeed in the building, but musket balls have been recovered at Cressing Temple Barns during archaeological digs. This evidence may also support the claim that the ghostly Hall Man is indeed Thomas Davies, this may be the reason why the spectral Cavalier carries a powder horn to charge his musket.

Another spirit that roams the grounds also met a tragic end at the barns. As late as the 1930s the Barley Barn and the Wheat Barn were penned and divided into rooms and hoppers. These compartments were made to create thrashing floors. A thrashing floor was used in order to fit as much crop as possible into the space available. This was achieved by bringing an old horse into the barn and walking it around to compress the wheat or barley. As the room filled up the horse would rise on top of the crop until it was eventually hoisted out of the room via a block and tackle. During one of these lifts a horse became agitated and kicked out. An unfortunate ostler, who was assisting with lifting the horse, was hit by the kick; the

The Barley Barn. (Photograph by Jason Day)

horses hoof hitting him in the head and killing him instantly. Depending on which eyewitness accounts you choose to believe the phantom ostler is said to haunt either of the Great Barns at Cressing Temple.

The final ghost that resides at Cressing Temple Barns was witnessed on several occasions by Frank Cullen, who owned the estate from 1912 until his death in 1967. During a visit to the barns in 1993, Michael Cullen recalled the accounts that his Great Uncle had related to him in an interview with Ian Mason, the educational officer at the site on the time. Michael Cullen said that Frank had talked to him about a ghost that would manifest itself to him on demand. During dinner one evening in the Oak room of the farm house, a guest asked Frank Cullen about the spirits that were believed to haunt the building. Frank replied that a ghost would be along in a few minutes. Sure enough, just before 9 p.m., unexplained noises were heard coming from behind the panelling in the oak room. One theory behind the identity of this spirit is that the obedient ghost was a man who lost his partner in a fire that occurred on the estate hundreds of years ago.

The Anguished Nun – Former Convent Building, Witham Road, Cressing

In late September 2006, workmen were carrying out some refurbishment work at a former convent on Witham Road, just outside of Braintree. Throughout their time there the workers were confronted with sporadic outbursts of paranormal activity.

The Wheat Barn roof. (Photograph by Kelly Day)

The men reported equipment unaccountably being moved around the site and hearing footsteps on the staircase, even though no one was on the stairs at the time.

One member of staff encountered the apparition of a nun who was crying out in agony. The unfortunate man was so terrified by the encounter that he immediately put down his tools and fled the building, refusing to return to work.

The Faulkbourne Cyclist – Faulkbourne Road, Faulkbourne near Witham

William the Conqueror handed the Manor of Faulkborne to his nephew following the Norman Conquest. The Manor was in possession of various families over the centuries, including the Fortescues. In 1637, the Fortescues sold the Hall to Sir Edward Bullock and the Bullock family (including Colonel John Bullock, Member of Parliament for Maldon from 1754 to 1774) lived at Faulkbourne until the late 1800s. The main residence, Faulkbourne Hall, was acquired in 1897 by the Parker family, who still live there.

Faulkbourne Hall dates back from around 1440 and is a red-bricked building with turrets and incorporates an earlier Norman tower. It has been suggested that a Roman villa originally stood on the site. There have been later additions and extensions to the property in the seventeenth and nineteenth centuries.

There has been local talk of the property being haunted for several years; however, reports extend out as far as the

Faulkbourne Hall estate itself and beyond. Faulkbourne Road, which passes the hall, has had several reports of a phantom cyclist. The apparition is described as a gentleman in a billycock hat riding an old fashioned bicycle. A billycock hat is a variant of a bowler hat and was popular *circa* 1850; coupled with the description of the cycle, it is fair to assume that the spirit is of a man from around that era.

Witnesses who have themselves been cycling along Faulkbourne Road describe the cyclist as having charged straight towards them. The belief is that his intention is to knock other cyclists off their bicycles, only the apparition disappears before there is any collision. Accounts also inform us that the phantom is usually seen at dusk and has no lights illuminating his advance.

Who is the Ghost of Feering All Saints? – All Saints' Church, Feering

All Saints' Church in Feering dates back to the thirteenth century and was later rebuilt in brick around AD 1500. The stone altar, which was built in 1961 by two parishioners, contains fragments from the ruins of Coggeshall Abbey, Walsingham Abbey and Colne Priory. The apparition of a man was regularly seen near a wall by a pulpit in the church during the 1890s. The mystery of who this man was may be just as intriguing as his ghostly appearances.

The story goes that the spirit is the ghost of John Hardman, a soldier killed in the Zulu war who was buried at Feering All Saints' Church. A search of the churchyard reveals no gravestone bearing John

All Saints' Church, Feering. (Photograph by Kelly Day)

All Saints' Church graveyard, Feering. (Photograph by Kelly Day)

Hardman's name, although some of the stones have had their engraving erased by time and the weather. There is also no record of a John Hardman fighting in the Zulu wars in Africa.

There are records of a John Harman however. John Harman(No. 678) was a member of the 1st Battalion of the 24th (2nd Warwickshire) Regiment of Foot. Harman served in Africa during the Zulu wars and was killed at the Battle of Isandhlwana Hill on 22 January 1879. Perhaps there has been some 'mix up' during the telling of the story over the years. If so, the question still remains as to who the ghostly man seen to be holding a bloody stomach wound in the church is? Is the ghost John Hardman and his history has been confused with somebody else's? Or is the ghost John Harman and for some reason he is haunting

Feering church? Could it be that the apparition is neither of these men and is another lost soul looking to rest in peace?

The Hatfield Road Ghost – A12, Hatfield Peverel

As an experienced lorry driver, Gary had heard many a story of spooky happenings on the roads from his colleagues over the years. Having had no such experiences himself, he had simply laughed them off.

One evening, he was travelling along the A12 near Hatfield Peverel, a journey he made six times a night, five nights a week. It was 2.20 a.m. and there was no other traffic in sight. Suddenly a man appeared to the side of Gary's vehicle and walked out directly in front of him. Gary slammed on his brakes but it was too late. He hit the man head on. Gary jumped out of his lorry and ran around the front. There was no sign of the man. There was no damage to his truck and no sign of any blood, in fact there was no evidence of the incident ever having occurred! Gary searched the area for a while and eventually continued his journey. Following his encounter his heart was pounding and he was shaking for a full thirty minutes afterwards.

He described the man as being in his late-forties to early-fifties, wearing an old style 'donkey jacket' and being 'scrunched up' as if he was very cold.

Gary now has a very different opinion of road ghosts and those that have encountered them. Being very shaken by his own experience he is now sorry to have not taken his colleagues stories so seriously.

Shaen's Shaggy Dog – Crix House, Hatfield Peverel

Six miles north-east of Chelmsford a creature known as 'Shaen's Shaggy Dog' was said to terrorise the village of Hatfield Peverel. On the Chelmsford side of the village stood a house called Crix, which was owned by the Shaen family from 1770 to 1858. The black dog is said to have roamed around the entrance gates to the property's driveway. There have been several reported instances of paranormal phenomena occurring around sightings of the creature and many have resulted in bizarre disappearances and even death.

A carter who encountered the hound is said to have come to a most unusual end. The large black dog blocked his side of the country lane and would not move. Wanting to chase the dog out of the way, the carter attempted to hit the dog, striking it with his riding crop. Upon doing so he was then immediately struck by a bolt of lightening. He was later found burnt to ashes next to his abandoned horse and wagon. Others who have reported seeing the black dog vanishing have subsequently returned to the spot and found scorched marks on the ground and a heavy smell of brimstone. Sightings of the hound became so frequent that the villagers accepted the creature as a matter of fact and, following some of their neighbours untimely demises, they wisely decided that it was best to leave the creature to its own devices and so he continued padding away until a fateful day early in the 1900s. A new invention, the motor car, had found its way onto the quiet lanes of rural Essex. A motorist reported seeing the hound as he drove into the village street. He saw the creature's eyes as he approached it. Just as the motorist drew level, the dog let out a piteous wail and exploded into a mass of flames and has never been seen since.

Silas and the Mean Spirit – Vinehurst House, The Street, Hatfield Peverel

Vinehurst, or Vinehurst House, located on The Street in Hatfield, Peverel, has a long and interesting history. The original building was an open hall structure built in the fourteenth century and was known as Vinehurst Cottage. The house was altered in the sixteenth and nineteenth centuries, becoming a much grander two storey property. Vinehurst still retains part of its original fourteenth-century roof and is now a Grade II listed building.

During the 1900s, there were reports that Vinehurst was undergoing a period

Vinehurst House, Hatfield Peverel. (Photograph by Jason Day)

of paranormal activity. There were said to be cold spots around the house that would herald the arrival of a spirit. The family dog would also become upset and agitated just before the unexplained temperature drops occurred. This particular spirit was said to be accompanied by a feeling of anxiety that spread to those who encountered it and may well have had a malevolent agenda.

A second, more benign, entity was also believed to be haunting the property at the time. This particular soul was said to be much friendlier, so much so that he was even given the name Silas by the residents of the house at the time.

With the William Boosey pub next door also being haunted, perhaps the spirits at Vinehurst House were visitors from 'next-door'.

The Phantom Pusher – William Boosey Public House, The Street, Hatfield Peverel

The William Boosey is a pub conveniently situated just off the A12 in the small village of Hatfield Peverel. It retains many original features, such as heavy oak beams and has a function room, beer garden and covered terrace. The pub is named after William Boosey who was its first landlord over 300 years ago and may also be the one of the alleged spirits that is said to haunt the establishment.

Since the early 2000s there have been reports that at least three entities are alleged to haunt the pub, with paranormal activity ranging from cold spots to unexplained sounds. The staff have also claimed to have

The William Boosey pub. (Photograph by Jason Day)

been pushed by unseen hands whilst working behind the bar. Some believe that William Boosey may still be trying to 'crack the whip' from beyond the grave.

The Disappearing Man – A12, Kelvedon

In July 1988, 22-year-old French trucker, Didier Chassagrande, was driving his lorry along the A12 in Kelvedon. Tragically, he hit a cyclist who then went under his 38 ton DAF articulated lorry. Didier jumped out of his truck and found the elderly, grey haired man who was bloody and unconscious. He dragged him and his mangled cycle to the side of the road and then ran off to seek help.

Didier reported the accident to the police and returned with them to the scene of the accident ten minutes later. After searching the area both the police and the horrified truck driver were astonished to learn that the old man and his bicycle had vanished. All that remained was the damage to the truck.

Does the former landlord still frequent his old haunt? (Photograph by Jason Day)

Sir John and the Monks – Beeleigh Abbey, Maldon

Beeleigh Abbey was constructed in 1180 and obtained a royal charter from Richard I in 1189. During the thirteenth century, the heart of Saint Roger of Beeleigh (a thirteenth-century Bishop of London) was buried at Beeleigh and the abbey became a pilgrimage site. In 1289, pilgrims included King Edward I and Queen Eleanor.

After the Dissolution of the monasteries, many of the abbey buildings were pulled down. In 1540, Henry VIII granted the abbey and lands to Sir John Gate,

Chancellor of the Duchy of Lancaster and High Sheriff of Essex. Sir John was involved in the plot to put Lady Jane Grey on the throne during the succession to the throne crisis in 1553. On 14 July 1553, Gates led the troops of the royal household to East Anglia in the campaign against Mary Tudor. He was arrested with Northumberland at Cambridge and tried at Westminster Hall on 19 August 1553. On 22 August 1553, he was beheaded at the Tower of London for treason. Towards the end of the 1500s there was an extension added to the abbey of a farmhouse.

During the eighteenth century, the building was used as a public house. By the late-nineteenth century, Beeleigh was being used as a farmhouse, the buildings were in a ruinous condition, but in 1912, restoration was begun by Captain F.W. Grantham. In 1943, the Abbey was purchased by William Foyle, owner of Foyles bookshop. The abbey is now a private residence and is not open to the public.

Whilst sleeping at the abbey one evening a former owner was woken at 3 a.m. by what they described as hands shaking the bed. She then began experiencing pains in her arm that required medical attention the following morning. The doctor that attended the patient described the injury to her arm as not unlike a bite from a tropical insect. Other people have reported feeling a sense of being watched whilst in the same room and one member of staff described seeing a ghostly hooded monk stood in the bedroom. A trapdoor was also found opened one morning, although it had been closed by a member of staff the night before. Recently, an excavation in the abbey grounds unearthed two unidentified skeletons at the bottom of a pond. Perhaps one of these sets of remains belongs to the monk that haunts the building.

Another spirit who is said to haunt the house is Sir John Gates himself. His ghost is believed to be responsible for the occasional unearthly screams heard throughout the abbey.

The White Lady – Maldon East Station Building, Station Road, Maldon

During the mid-1800s, Maldon had two railway stations: Maldon West and Maldon East. The stations were located at either end of the site of the current Maldon Bypass. The Maldon West station's track ran under the Spital Road and the bridge that was built to accommodate the line is still visible from where the goods yard once was. During the Second World War, the passenger services on the Maldon West to Woodham Ferrers line was withdrawn as an economy measure and never reinstated. Following the war, the line continued to be used for goods traffic but with nationalisation of the railways it was completely closed in 1953. What was the goods yard of the station is now an industrial estate, with only one old brick built shed remaining as testament to the sites former occupants.

The first goods trains left Maldon's other station (Maldon East) in August 1948, with passenger services soon following. The Maldon East line continued passenger traffic until 1964 when this service was withdrawn. The station continued goods services for a further two years, transporting canned food and agricultural machinery, until 1966 when the station closed completely.

The first documented reports of paranormal activity regarding the railways emerged during the late-1950s and seemed to gravitate around Maldon East Station and the surrounding area. The most

The former Maldon East Station building that now houses offices. (Photograph by Jason Day)

common phenomena reported by staff at the station were the sightings of an apparition of a white lady. Witnesses claimed that the temperature would fall dramatically on platform 2 of the station, immediately before the spirit would manifest itself. The sound of an eerie, wailing woman was also heard emanating from the vicinity of platform 2 during cold, dark nights. A rational explanation was never found for the cries. One station master was so petrified by the occurrences at Maldon East Station that he took to sleeping with a loaded shotgun under his pillow. The phenomena continued throughout the station's service and reports extended into the mid-1970s, nine years after the trains had stopped running from the station.

Following the closure of the line, Maldon East Station fell into disrepair until two local business men decided to take the derelict building and turn it into a public house and restaurant. During renovations, builders discovered a damp patch of soil beneath the former station's floorboards. Disturbingly, the shape of the damp patch seemed to resemble the shape of an adult, human figure. The builders dug the patch up only to find that the shape re-appeared in the soil. Following several repercussions of this phenomena the builders decided to leave the soil as it was and continue their work.

With repairs on the building completed, the former Maldon East Station re-opened its doors in 1974 beginning its new life as the 'Great Eastern' pub and restaurant. Almost immediately staff and customers reported strange experiences within the building. There were regular reports of unexplainable temperature drops and unaccountable noises on the premises. At least one witness claimed to have seen a 'white misty form' near the washrooms in the pub. Some staff became so traumatised by what they experienced at the building that they even quit their jobs rather than deal with the spirit or spirits that resided there. Had the white lady returned to her old haunt? The 'Great Eastern' closed two years later in 1976.

The station is now a listed building and houses offices which incorporate the old platform. Whether the white lady will make her presence known to the current residents remains to be seen.

The Phantoms of Moot Hall – Moot Hall, High Street, Maldon

It is believed that the Moot Hall in Maldon was constructed in the 1420s and was originally built for the D'Arcy family. The Hall eventually became a seat for power in the town and from 1810 housed a courtroom, which served as both a Magistrate's Court and a Court of Quarter Sessions; in the former role, it was still in use until 1950.

From 1863 until 1900, the ground floor was used as Maldon's police station and prison. Several cells were divided by partitions and iron grills. One such grill in the interior door is witness to its former use. The position of the partitions can be seen in the walls by the existence of replaced brickwork. At the back of the hall there is a small exercise yard used by the prisoners, which still displays examples of Victorian graffiti scratched into the brickwork of the walls.

A White Lady is said to walk the old station platform. (Photograph by Jason Day)

The cellar at Moot Hall, Maldon. (Photograph by Jason Day)

The staircase to the court room at Moot Hall, Maldon. (Photograph by Jason Day)

The hall also houses a council chamber and a clock tower on the roof. Although the court room, exercise yard, council chambers and many other features still remain, Moot Hall is no longer used for 'official' purposes. The hall is now a mixture of a museum, events venue and home to its very own ghosts.

Tour guides at the hall describe hearing footsteps when there is nobody else in the building and experiencing the feeling of being watched. Guides also frequently report seeing shadowy figures gliding from room to room. In the past, the hall regularly played host to paranormal investigations and many attendees reported similar experiences to the guides. There have also been incidents where doors on the upper levels have slammed shut when no one was near them and people hearing banging on walls, disembodied voices and breathing. During vigils on a paranormal investigation in 2009, an unexplained foul stench was reported emanating from the judges chambers. No source could be found for the smell at the time and no explanation for this unusual phenomenon has been found since. One of the most interesting incidents at the hall was the sighting of a phantom figure seen walking across the exercise yard.

The identity of the spirits of Moot Hall is unknown. Perhaps they are former policemen or officials that worked at the old police station or court room, still performing their duties, or maybe they could be disgruntled inmates, fated to serve eternity in the old cells.

The Maldon Poltergeist –
The Kings Head, High Street, Maldon

The Kings Head pub in Maldon pre-dates the 1500s. The building has been extended several times over the past 300 years and it is these renovations that may well have caused some of the paranormal activity that is said to have occurred on the premises.

Poltergeist activity was reported at the pub during Christmas 1946, when a couple staying there were subjected to hearing phantom footsteps outside their room and being trapped by an unknown force that held their bedroom door closed. Other phenomena that has occurred at the Kings Head includes objects being moved from room to room with no apparent human aid, eventually being found in various different doorways around the building. Mysterious footsteps have also been heard running across hallways and up and down stairs. Another unfortunate visitor was unexpectedly trapped in the upstairs lavatory despite the door being easy to open and close upon inspection.

During one of the spells of renovation at the pub a gruesome discovery was made; dozens of human bones were found beneath some floorboards that were taken up. It is believed that the pub itself was built over the remains of an old plague pit and that the remains may belong to some of the poor souls that died during these horrific times.

The King's Head, Maldon. The pub was the home of the infamous 'Maldon Poltergeist' during the 1940s. (Photograph by Jason Day)

Even more harrowing are the rumours that a former landlord of the pub was a scheming serial killer who preyed on wealthy travellers. The remains, it is said, may indeed be those of his victims, finally uncovered, revealing his foul deeds.

Whether the spirits that haunt the Kings Head are indeed plague victims or victims of a murderous landlord is unsure. Further investigation by paranormal groups or psychic mediums may uncover more details in the future.

The Ghostly Arm and the Phantom Children – Town Hall, Newlands Street, Witham

The Town Hall has always been one of the most important buildings in Witham and has had a very interesting and chequered past. Parts of the structure of the hall can be dated back to the fourteenth century, when the building was a coaching Inn.

The George Inn, as it was known then, stands on the town's high street, Newland Street. Newland Street lies exactly on the path of the old Roman Road and as such was of significant importance to those travelling or transporting goods by coach. This meant that The George, and several other coaching inns, flourished during this period of Witham's history.

During the seventeenth century, The George developed something of a reputation for 'admitting unlawful assemblies upon the Sabbath day, spending their time drinking, playing and the like at the time of divine service'. It was also the centre of violent disputes in Newland Street,

Witham Town Hall. (Photograph by Jason Day)

The main entrance to the Hall takes you through into the gift shop. (Photograph by Jason Day)

between the town's people and Irish soldiers billeted locally. Its fortunes changed in the eighteenth century with the success of the passing coach trade, and by the 1780s the premises included:

> [...]a spacious assembly room, large and small dining parlours, good bed chambers, wine vaults and beer cellars, a complete brewing office, stabling for upwards of 70 horses with good hay and granaries, coach house, a garden well stocked with every convenience that is fitting for an inn.

In the 1800s, the building became a bank and in 1993 the building was purchased by the Town Council. A lengthy refurbishment began and the building became the Town Hall, housing a Heritage Centre which was opened in May 1995, and the ever increasingly popular Tourist Information Centre.

During a visit to the Town Hall in 2011, I discovered there may also be something of a more paranormal nature housed within its walls. A member of staff related to me that there had been several unexplained occurrences on the ground floor of the building, particularly along a corridor that leads from a function room to the Tourist Information Centre and gift shop. The sounds of children's voices have been heard around the area of the corridor that leads to a staircase down to the cellar. These voices are heard despite the fact that there are no children around at the time.

The most startling piece of evidence pertaining to paranormal activity in the building, involved the member of staff I spoke to. The woman was walking along the corridor in question when an arm extended out from a small corridor, one that branched off from the main corridor to the left. As this small corridor led to the Tourist Information Centre and gift shop the witness assumed it was a colleague making their way from the shop. As she turned to enter the small corridor she discovered there was nobody there. The witness opened the closed door to the gift shop and found her colleague in there. She asked whether her colleague or anybody else had just left the room and entered the small corridor, to which she was told no.

With a history spanning nearly 500 years surely it is inevitable that the Town Hall should remain a home to some of the spirits that may have visited or resided there during their time in this world.

The Forgotten Tunnels – Spring Lodge Community Centre, Powers Hall End, Witham

Spring Lodge is a community centre located on the Powers Hall End road in Witham. The community centre opened in 1973 and consists of a reception area, bar and five rooms used for meetings, clubs and lectures. There are three smaller rooms, one of which is used for a pre-school/nursery, a main hall, complete with stage, and another hall which is a converted barn.

The barn itself was built in the sixteenth century and appears to be the hub that the rest of the centre was built around. It may also be that the barn is the centre of the alleged paranormal activity that is said to occur in the building.

In the past, members of staff have reported seeing the figure of a small child, in several locations around the building; even up amongst the old wooden beams in the barn, which is now known as hall five. Members of staff have also reported arriving for work and entering the pre-school/nursery room to find toys and furniture strewn around the room. They were astonished as to how this could have occurred because the room had been tidied before the building was locked up the previous evening. Some of the witnesses say it is the spirit of the small child, believed to be a girl, who plays with the toys in the pre-school/nursery during the night.

There is another spectre that has, on at least one occasion, been seen wandering the hallways of Spring Lodge. During the early 2000s, a dark figure was seen in the hallway outside the barn by a member of staff. The figure is said to have resembled a monk and was only visible from the head down to mid-thigh level. As the apparition floated along it appeared to have no lower legs or feet.

A caretaker at the community centre has relayed many unusual events to me, including unexplained shadows and sounds within the building. Local legend has it that the barn had ties to nearby St Nicholas Church on Chipping Hill, which is less than a mile away from Spring Lodge. The two locations were said to be connected by underground tunnels which are now believed to no longer exist. Perhaps the tunnels were constructed for holy men to make a hasty escape to the barn during the times of the Reformation in England. This could explain the ghostly presence of the monk that now inhabits the former barn.

Bibliography

Books

Christmas, Harry, George Augustus and Frederick Fitzclarence, *The Literary Gazette*, Vol. 8
(H.Colburn, 1824)

Cox, J. Charles, *Parish Registers of England*, (London, Methuen & Co. Ltd, First Published in 1910)

Day, Jason, *Paranormal Essex*, (Stroud, The History Press, 2011)

King, Carmel, *Haunted Essex*, (Stroud, The History Press, 2009)

Payne, Jessie K., *A Ghost Hunters Guide to Essex*, (Essex, Ian Henry Publications Ltd, 1987)

Price, Harry, *Poltergeist Over England: Three Centuries Of Mischievous Ghosts*, (London, Country Life Ltd, 1945)

Newspapers, Magazines and Journals

A true relation of a horrid murder committed upon the person of Thomas Kidderminster, of Tupsley in the county
of Hereford, Gent., at the White-Horse Inn in Chelmsford, in the county of Essex, in the month of April, 1654
(Pamphlet, 1688)

'COGGESHALL: Chef Mark Baumann may call in ghost hunters to brasserie', *Essex Chronicle*
(16 September 2010)

Crouch, Barry J. 'Cressing Temple Barns Archive Report' (http//:cressingtemple.org.uk/ghosts/
CTsecret.htm – information is researched from archived material as it appeared on the website on
January 29 2009)

Dawson, Ian, 'The Witch and the Stone', *Ash Magazine*, Issue No. 2, (1988)

Durr, Peter, 'The Little Leighs Body Snatchers' *Essex Police Museum 'History Notebook'*, Issue No.51.

Essex Countryside, Vol.12, No.89 (June 1964)

Essex Review, Vol XXLX, No. 16 (October 1920)

Essex Weekly News (February 1946 & June 1952)

'Foreign News: On Scrapfaggot Green', *Times Magazine* (Monday October 23 1944)

'Is Dead Owner Haunting His Restaurant?', *Daily Gazette* (8 September 2010)

Morgan, Nina, 'Ghosts Pose for Camera', *Braintree and Witham Times* (4 February 2011)

Rowley, Sheila, *Little Baddow: The History of an Essex Village,* (Booklet, 1975)

Saunders, Keiron, 'By gum! Flattened cyclist vanishes', *The Sun* newspaper (15 July 1988)

The Times (5 January 1824)

The Morning Chronicle (19 January 1824)

White, Alison, 'Spirit Searches' *Paranormal Magazine* (December 2006)

Websites

www.baumannsbrasserie.co.uk

www.chelmsford.gov.uk

Essex Ghost Hunting Team – essexghosthunting.webs.com

www.essexwalks.com

www.francisfrith.com

www.ghostsandstories.com

www.greenwayentertainment.com

www.itsaboutmaldon.co.uk

Jason Day's Official Website – www.jasonday.co.uk

www.oldenglishinns.co.uk/coggeshal

www.paranormal database.com

Peter Underwood – www.peterunderwood.org.uk

www.pubsinuk.com

www.rootschat.com/forum

The Society For Psychical Research – www.spr.ac.uk

www.stannescastle.co.uk

www.suite101.com

Tracie Wayling – www.traciewayling.com

www.vintageinn.co.uk/theangelbroomfield

www.websuite.co.uk

White Noise Paranormal Radio – www.whitenoiseparanormalradio.co.uk

If you enjoyed this book, you may also be interested in ...

Haunted Scunthorpe

JASON DAY

From the 1700s and the most documented poltergeist case in history, to the family hom
currently experiencing a third generation of paranormal activity, *Haunted Scunthorpe*
guides you through the town's paranormal hotspots and follows the apparitions into th
surrounding villages and beyond. Including previously unpublished haunting accounts
from the author's own case files, this collection of local hauntings and has something fc
everyone, from the layman to the hardened paranormal investigator.

978 0 7524 5521 1

Haunted Grimsby

JASON DAY

Haunted Grimsby features all manner of spectres – from the ghosts of the past to the hauntin
of the present. Visit the hotel haunted by shadowy children and the shop plagued by a
malevolent presence; climb aboard the vessel manned by phantom crewmen and tour the
museum with a ghostly guide. Jason Day is an expert on paranormal research, the director
of a paranormal events company, and a radio host with his own show discussing all things
supernatural. He has written countless articles on the subject for various magazines.

978 0 7524 6056 7

Paranormal Essex

JASON DAY

Take a tour around one of England's oldest and most paranormally active counties. Visi
the site of the 'Most Haunted House In England' at Borley, encounter the mysterious
Spider of Stock, witness an RAF pilot's shocking near miss with a UFO over the skies
of Southend, and find out about the infamous 'Witchfinder General'. With an extensiv
collection of paranormal reports includes previously unpublished accounts from the
author's personal case files. *Paranormal Essex* will delight all lovers of the unexplained.

978 0 7524 5527 3

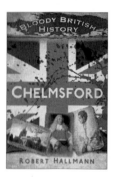

Bloody British History: Chelmsford

ROBERT HALLMANN

Chelmsford has one of the darkest histories on record. From the skeletons lying
underneath the city – which include a woolly mammoth – to the executions of thieve
witches, martyrs and murderers at Chelmsford's gaol, this book will change the way yo
see the town forever. Robert the Bruce was most likely born here; Bloody Mary Tudo
lived here; infamous murderers Samuel Dougal and Thomas Drory died here. Including
more than sixty rare illustrations.

978 0 7524 7115 0

Visit our website and discover thousands of other History Press books.
www.thehistorypress.co.uk